MORE>
Truth
Searching for certainty in an uncertain world.

Kristi Mair

INTER-VARSITY PRESS
36 Causton Street, London SW1P 4ST, England
Email: ivp@ivpbooks.com
Website: www.ivpbooks.com

First published 2019

British Library Cataloguing-in-Publication Data
A catalogue record for this book is available from the British Library.

ISBN: 978-1-78359-766-6
eBook ISBN: 978-1-78359-767-3

Set in Bembo 10.5/15 pt
Typeset in Great Britain by CRB Associates, Potterhanworth, Lincolnshire
Printed in Great Britain by Ashford Colour Press Ltd, Gosport, Hampshire

Inter-Varsity Press publishes Christian books that are true to the Bible and that communicate the gospel, develop discipleship and strengthen the church for its mission in the world.

IVP originated within the Inter-Varsity Fellowship, now the Universities and Colleges Christian Fellowship, a student movement connecting Christian Unions in universities and colleges throughout Great Britain, and a member movement of the International Fellowship of Evangelical Students. Website: www.uccf.org.uk. That historic association is maintained, and all senior IVP staff and committee members subscribe to the UCCF Basis of Faith.

To the Book my mother reads

Contents

I am the way
and the *truth*
and the life.

(John 14:6, emphasis added)

Introduction

THE QUEST FOR TRUTH

Truth is an uncomfortable word. A trigger. Like 'politics' or 'religion', 'truth' is often brought up in order to have the final say in Starbucks over our soya flat whites. It's the ultimate trump card. Appealing to 'the truth' rarely creates conversations; more often it closes them down. That is the nature of inflexible, overarching claims of truth. All we see are hard edges, no rounded corners. And no wonder. While we want truth, we live in a confused world which tells us to fear it.

As the adage goes, 'the most certain are the most dangerous'. We could even change it to, 'the more intolerant the "truth", the more dangerous it becomes'. Paris, London, Manchester, 9/11, 7/7: these are all awful examples of the violence produced by inflexible beliefs. ISIS and other extremist groups epitomize the danger of truth claims. They are dangerous because they are arrogant and willing to act in accordance with their certainty. This is one side of the truth-coin, the side that makes us want to run from ultimate, inflexible, black-and-white truth.

And yet, there is another side. For better or worse, we still desire truth. We do not want to be misled. We do not want to be deceived. From politicians to celebrities, we feel betrayed when sources of authority let us down. We want credible truth claims that we can act upon confidently, and we would love to know that what we hear is the truth, to weigh it and find it not wanting. But what if we don't have the time, energy or ability to weigh each and every statement flooding out of the White House or Russia, news networks or social media? Elections are won and lost on such things. Or are they? Who can say?

Welcome to the world of post-truth. You can identify its impact in the weariness printed across our foreheads. We are tired. Tired of hearing everybody's truth just to be misled. Tired of wondering what truth is and whether it's even possible to know something truly. But something in us just can't give up. When human rights activists take up their placards and, due to public outrage, political protestors flood town squares, we soon see that no matter who we are, truth matters. Something deep within us calls for truth. Whether we are artists, cleaners, doctors, lawyers, musicians, linguists, writers, we all want to know the truth.

And as Christians, we claim to have found it. Or, rather, *him*.

Nearly 2,000 years ago, one evening after dinner, a penniless rabbi from the backwater of Nazareth said to his friends, 'I am the way and the *truth*, and the life' (John 14:6, emphasis added). Christians claim that this outrageous assertion changes lives even today. Yet, how can it be taken seriously in our post-truth society? In a time when tribal consensus takes precedence over evidence or facts, what Jesus says is seismic. He says he *is* The Truth. He *is* the epicentre of all truthful activity.

Ever since they were uttered, these words have been hotly disputed. Jesus warned his disciples that the world – sinful humanity – would hate them for belonging to the truth (John 15:19) because truth renders all who don't believe in him wrong. Truth divides. Still. How dare we say there is one truth? Everyone has a right to decide and live out their own. Jesus' claim to be The Truth is as shocking today as it was when it was first spoken. It provokes a variety of questions: Can this be true? How do we know? Is it even *possible* to live in the truth? Jesus calls us to follow him; what does it look like for us to walk in the truth? And, finally, how on earth can we be truth-tellers in a society that says, 'I'll respect your truth if you respect mine'? How do we speak the truth of Christ into weary post-truth apathy?

The stakes couldn't be higher. For how we receive, respond to and relay truth fundamentally affects how we relate to God, others and ourselves. My prayer is that this book will help to dismantle preconceptions so that we can re-evaluate truth, equipping ourselves to engage with rather than withdraw from debates about truth, that we'll enjoy the freedom of truth in Jesus and, most of all, that we will be shaped into a counter-cultural community of Truth-lovers.

'Did God really say, "You must not eat from any tree in the garden"?'

(Genesis 3:1–2)

Chapter one

TWISTING TRUTH – A GARDEN OF LIES

'You go to church? So you actually believe in God, then?' I imagine many of you have been faced with this question, perhaps with a beer in your hand and music pulsing in the background.

You nod.

'That's nice,' your friend says.

You rack your brains as to how to answer. 'Mmm, I think it's nice because it's true,' you reply.

'Truth? Ha, what *is* truth?' the questioner responds with a broad grin.

It's a good question – a big question, one that has occupied some of the greatest minds in history. And yet, not all of history, for there was once a time when humans undoubtedly knew they were walking in the truth.

They were walking in a garden – with Truth himself.

BACK TO THE BEGINNING

In our exploration for truth it makes sense to start at the beginning. It starts in a garden. There are two people. A man and a woman – Adam and Eve – and they are in the most luscious surroundings they could ever have imagined. Not that they needed to imagine. *It was*. And it was good.

Things are going well. They are enjoying eating from the tree of life, hanging with the animals. Eve continues to tease Adam for naming that large, grey thing a 'hippopotamus'. It really was not good for him to be alone! But even the two of them together are not alone; God lives with them, and all his heavenly counsel. Eden is home, and they both want and need for nothing. They are with God. With each other. Knowing him and being known by him. Real intimacy. Real truth.

Then one day, Eve starts chatting with one of these celestial beings. He asks her questions: 'Did God really say . . .?' She answers him, starts to doubt and, most catastrophically, she turns from truth: she lies (see opposite).

God never banned touching the tree back in Genesis 2:17. Something exceptionally sad and uniquely severe has happened. Eve has questioned God's character and his generosity. She has used her reason against God. Before she even takes a bite, she does nothing to resist the snare of the serpent. As he winds his way

'Did God really say, "You must not eat from any tree in the garden"?' The woman said to the serpent, 'We may eat fruit from the trees in the garden, but God did say, "You must not eat fruit from the tree that is in the middle of the garden, and you must not touch it, or you will die."'

(Genesis 3:1–3)

around that supposed tree, sin is twisting its way around Eve's heart. And so, she eats. And she falls. And without a second thought she passes the fruit on to Adam. He has been there the whole time. Silent. He heard it all and said nothing, *did* nothing. If anything, he is more culpable because he is the one to whom God had first revealed the garden's terms and conditions. Despite knowing and seeing all of that, he too eats. And he too falls.

As they do, a barrier is built between them and ultimate truth. They are barred and blocked by God, their creator. Evil has corrupted them. They no longer have the truth. The tree of life is off limits. The Truth that gave them life, satisfied their souls with good things and walked with them, in justice, kicks them out. The consequence of curses hits them hard. Immediate spiritual death and eventual physical death is now their truth.

Those events in the garden reverberate today. For many, a brief moment of truth is all we can taste – a piece of music moves us, the glory of nature stuns us, for a moment pointing beyond, to something more, to truth, to a Creator – but then it is gone and we are left wanting, left searching for something to satisfy that hunger. All humanity has fallen in Adam, and we continue to pass on the putrefying fruit of sin, hoping that what we eat, what we do, what we think will enable us to 'be like God'. But, in reality, we are left in ruins.

Humanity knew Truth and we did not want him. We broke God's Word, his law in Genesis 2:17, and, as we did, we rejected relationship with him. Law-breaking is relational. From Adam and Eve to this very day, humanity has wanted to de-create God, the uncreated one, so that we could be made more: more like God (3:5).

As God was dethroned, self was enthroned – sin winding around our hearts, giving us a distorted view of our place in the world. We exchanged the *truth* for a *lie*, making ourselves arbiters of truth, not God. We now decide what constitutes good and evil – we twisted the truth, and we continue to twist it. This is the reality many live with today. And yet, this isn't the end. The story doesn't end in the garden.

But blessed are your eyes because they see, and your ears because they hear. For truly I tell you, many prophets and righteous people longed to see what you see but did not see it, and to hear what you hear but did not hear it.

(Matthew 13:16–17)

Chapter two

TRACING TRUTH – A JOURNEY FOR TRUTH

The bestselling book of all time (no, not *Harry Potter*, the Bible) claims to tell the truth of Jesus Christ. But (spoiler alert) not everyone believes it. Maybe you're struggling to believe it yourself. Nevertheless, it is impossible to ignore the fact that humanity is a 'glorious ruin'. We see the disastrous effects of having walked away from truth all too easily, but we also harbour a relentless hope to find it again.

We see this disconnection from truth in the way the search to find it again has occupied the hearts and minds of many throughout the ages. Though we will look at what the words of Jesus mean for our current uncertain world, a brief navigation of this historical terrain will help us to understand our present situation – and truth itself – that bit better.

Whether we realize it or not, at heart, all of us are philosophers. This is because, at its simplest, philosophy has tried to answer the five big questions in life: *What is real? How do we know? Why are we here? Who am I? What is right and wrong?*

Naturally, these questions throw up much discussion and many different positions. This kind of dialogue is what philosophers live for. Some of my favourite times working with the Universities and Colleges Christian Fellowship have been when students and recent graduates have gathered in my lounge over whisky and wine to talk about these big questions late into the night. The chances are you have done this too. We are all philosophers. We are all pursuing wisdom of some kind.

Every generation has looked to different groups of people for answers. A previous generation went to the scientists for the answers to life's questions. Today it's more the popstar poets and Hollywood. But not so long ago, philosophers were *the* go-to authority. The theories we will look at below provide just a handful of personal and painful deliberations for truth without God, which form the foundation for the way many currently approach truth today.

A BRIEF HISTORY OF TRUTH

Philosophers have been exploring truth and where we can find it for thousands of years, but these three remain the most defining views of recent times: rationalism, empiricism and existentialism. For those hippopotomonstrosesquipedaliophobics (people with a fear of long words, ironically) among us, don't be put off: we encounter these foundations of thought day in, day out, as alternatives to biblical knowledge: it's likely that most people we know will hold one or a hodgepodge of these ways of thinking. Whether you consider yourself a 'deep thinker' or not, it is crucial for Christians to understand these alternatives to the 'truth' since, as we shall see, this will enable us to share our truth better with others.

Descartes's apples of rationalism

The year is 1641. We join Descartes in his sitting room. He is warming himself before a roaring fire and his mind begins to bend. Through self-reflection, a near transcendental experience, Descartes asks, 'How can I know anything?' This is a tricky question, especially after he'd had a couple of drinks (perhaps you've found yourself asking the same?).

He decides to peel back the layers of knowledge by removing everything he can doubt. This thought experiment is called Methodic Doubt. As he cannot be sure the apples in front of him exist, he removes them. How can he be sure that he isn't deceived by some kind of malicious demon, that the external world isn't one of smoke and mirrors? The Matrix trilogy taps into this thought beautifully. The apples in front of me may be a mere illusion, a false manifestation – and so they cannot be foundational to knowledge. A similar scepticism can hang over much of Christian thought and practice, for reasons we will see.

After a few tours on this philosophical trip, Descartes realizes that the only thing he cannot doubt is himself. In order to think, there must be the existence of the 'I' that is doing the thinking. This is the summation of his famous phrase 'cogito ergo sum': I am thinking, therefore, I am.

There are a couple of obvious problems with this, namely: Descartes walks into a bar. The bartender asks him if he'd like a drink. Descartes replies, 'I think not,' and he ceases to exist.

The implication is obvious – do we stop existing when we stop thinking? What Descartes's late-night thought experiment achieved was to cast doubt on our sense perception and what it means for us, as physical human beings, to encounter truth. Everything that can be doubted should be doubted. Adopting the above-down approach, Descartes believed it is by removing ourselves and looking down on problems and situations that we are able to see them most clearly, most objectively. Truth lies in objectivity and in the 'I' that is able to do the thinking. The sum total of what it means to know truth is reduced to our mental capacities. Existence is grounded in the objective self and, using deductive reason, he holds that reality has a rational structure to it and all knowledge can be assessed using logical principles.

In Descartes we see the need for personal truth, but without an external anchor of truth it can lead to absurdities. As we will see later, it is at this intersection between internal and external knowledge that Christ as Truth speaks.

Locke's empirical blank slate

Fast-forward twenty-five years and we see another school of thought circulating, empiricism, often personified in the long-nosed person of John Locke. He believed that we are born as a 'blank slate' (*tabula rasa*) that our sensory experience writes upon. How do we know anything? We know because we experience it directly. Rather than knowing things innately or by tradition, empiricists have a very high view of evidence, making it the founding father of the scientific method: all theories and hypotheses must be tested in the natural world by repeatable observation and experiment.

As if things weren't hard enough to think about, philosophers love to use Latin terms and long words. Don't be put off by this. The main thing is that we grasp the different ways of deciding what is true. It is not enough to appeal to self-evident propositions like $2 + 2 = 4$ (philosophers call this a priori knowledge), like Descartes did. We need evidence, that is knowledge based on observations or experience (a posteriori knowledge). We need to see that what you state to be true is indeed true.

It goes without saying that not all philosophers fit neatly into the rationalist or empirical camp. One of these people was Immanuel Kant (1724–1804), who chose to speak into both spheres. As far as Christianity is concerned, he has a lot to answer for. Kant's distinction between faith and reason, between the world of what is not known and the world that can be seen and investigated, is what has largely led to the sacred/secular divide of today. There are things, he says, we cannot know because they lie beyond experience; we cannot experience them through scientific testing. God and faith fall into this category. What we are left with is 'practical reason'. While we cannot prove or disprove the existence of God scientifically, we are free to employ our practical reason as moral beings and believe in God if we want to. Kant famously said that he wanted to limit science in order to make room for faith. You don't need to imagine the result: we are living in it today.

These totalizing systems, however, cannot quite account for reality, for what we know to be true. Kant, for example, speaks of a little something called 'mother wit' – a source of knowledge *outside* our reason. It is written in nature. He then quickly moves on. Scholars have chosen to look away, as acknowledging this would undo Kant's theory of knowledge entirely. This is vital. Truth may be available that we do not understand or perhaps even have access to via practical reason. The view 'that's your truth, here is mine' breaks down under this analysis. Truth is true regardless of personal consent.

Being and becoming the existentialists

Before we look at the impact these movements are having on the way people understand the gospel today, we need to spare a thought for the existentialists. Arising in the mid 1800s, they reached their zenith in the mid 1900s in France. Their motto is 'existence precedes essence'. Being is becoming. Far from the ultimate maker described in Psalm 139 knitting us together in our mother's womb, no man or woman possesses a fixed purpose at birth. Instead, each person is free to determine what they will be through their own rational choices and without the external constraints of societal or religious pressures. We give meaning, the essence, to our own existence, and it is up to us to live as 'authentically' as possible. Existential angst will be encountered along the way as we understand the burden of responsibility we have for our own lives through the choices we are to make in an irrational universe. This is something we may feel very acutely indeed. Appreciating the magnitude of life and the vastness of all we could be creates angst and fear, as we see that life is not what we had expected. The search for meaning took the existentialists within themselves. What is a good decision? It's up to you (as long as you don't act in bad faith and you do no harm).

But can existentialism *really* encapsulate all truth? Take this thought from the famous existentialist, Albert Camus: 'Beauty is unbearable, drives us to despair, offering us for a minute the glimpse of an eternity that we should like to stretch out over the whole of time.' A glimpse of eternity. Camus is pushing at the boundaries of his adopted world view here. He sees perfectly well where it leads and what it entails. How can the existentialist square the circle of what beauty seems to be pointing to, the longing it evokes, coupled with belief in the reality of a meaningless universe? It seems that to be true to existentialism, Camus has to deny that which seems to be innate – the experience of beauty pointing beyond itself. There is no beyond. It is all meaningless. To suppress that call of eternity is to deny the experience itself. And perhaps even Camus had to admit this was something he couldn't ignore, it being said that he came to Christ before the end of his life. As he probed the edges of existentialism, perhaps he allowed beauty to lead him to eternity.

THERE MUST BE MORE>

In their search for meaning, each one of these philosophers stumbles on something that cannot be boxed into their 'truth'. The same can be seen in the journals of nineteenth-century artist, Eugène Delacroix (see opposite).

Ever since sin entered the world and our relationship with truth became obscured, men and women have been scrambling, searching for the light, longing to discover it again. We have settled for false dichotomies: is meaning in us (existentialists) or outside us (empiricists)? Or, to put it differently (as classical philosophers might have done), is meaning up there or down here? The general trajectory has been a downward one. We have gone from the elevated principles of essences, change and forms, down to subjectivity, to the deciding self, the rule of 'me'. We have gone from an open universe to a closed universe, up (objectivity) to down (subjectivity). To a large extent, that is where we remain. And yet, as we will see, a longing for that 'happy dream' persists.

Could a mere chance combination of the elements have created the virtues, reflections of an unknown grandeur! If the universe had been produced by chance, what would conscience mean, or remorse, or devotion? O! if only, with all the strength of your being, you could believe in that God who invented duty, all your doubts and hesitations would be resolved. For why not admit it? It is always questions of this life, fears for it or for your comfort, that disturb your fleeting days – days that would slip by peacefully enough, if at the end of your journey you saw your Heavenly Father waiting to receive you! I must leave this and go to bed, but it has been a happy dream.

(Eugène Delacroix)

Dear children,
let us not love
with words or
speech but
with actions
and in truth.

(1 John 3:18)

Chapter three

TIMELY TRUTH – OUR CURRENT MOMENT

There was a time when calling someone 'sceptical' was a bit of a put down. We dreamers had no time for the Debbie Downers of life. But when you contrast it with being gullible, which would you rather be? In the wake of fake news and false claims, scepticism seems a morally praiseworthy position to adopt.

Philosophical scepticism questions our ability to know anything with certainty, and it is rife in our world today. It is perhaps no wonder then that Jesus' claim, the cornerstone of Christianity, that he is the 'Truth' – along with his healings and miraculous resurrection – is likely to get some people's backs up; even the most optimistic and friendly of sceptics. At its core, philosophical scepticism is seen as either having zero possibility of knowing anything at all or having to suspend all judgment and sit on the fence, because it isn't possible to know either way about anything. This scepticism has led to where we currently find ourselves: Christians claiming to know the ultimate truth in an ultimately post-truth society.

WHAT IS POST-TRUTH?

The word 'post-truth' has been used so often in the wake of the US election and the EU referendum that the *Oxford English Dictionary* declared it international word of the year in 2016. The *OED* defines post-truth as 'relating to or denoting circumstances in which objective facts are less influential in shaping public opinion than appeals to emotion and personal belief'. Post-truth means appealing to 'truth' won't help us persuade anyone. Society is beyond it, and so the swamp becomes even stickier to wade through when we think or talk about Jesus Christ as The Truth.

VIRTUE SIGNALLING

You may have seen the Channel 4 interview between Jordan Peterson and Cathy Newman discussing the gender pay gap. Newman wanted to make the point that the gender pay gap is deplorable and should be demolished. Peterson responded by articulating many reasons for the pay gap; gender is one of them, and a small contributing factor at that. Newman did not listen, instead demonstrating her virtue credentials as a woman who cares about the pay gap. And she evidently cares more than this man. She is, therefore, more virtuous than he is.

Virtue signalling is about being seen to say or do the 'right' thing and it's prevalent today. The chances are you've come across this often: news, social media, personal conversations. It is here that we see our scepticism at play: if no-one has access to truth (certain knowledge), then why believe the expert? They speak as though they want what they are saying to be true. It is not the language and tone of dry, detached academics; it is the language of vision. And it is powerful.

This disjunct between the 'elite' and the 'normal' can be seen starkly in the 2016 US elections. The people said, 'Washington doesn't work.' They wanted an outsider, someone who hadn't been corrupted by realpolitik. The Trump campaign appealed to moral and economic 'greatness', a powerful rallying cry for the farmer or factory-worker struggling to make ends meet. The 'suits' promised change but delivered little. Trump, however, will get the best deal for *you*. It's the 'suits' kind of propositional knowledge of facts and numbers that we are tempted to resist. After all, isn't there something deficient to truth if all it cares for is propositional statements? As we will see shortly, Jesus agrees.

SCEPTICISM LEADING TO CYNICISM

You're walking down a dark street alone and a person from a different demographic is walking towards you. Do you stop and get to know them? Do you quicken your pace to walk away? Ever since Eden, since our relationship with truth has been broken, we find ourselves living in *distrust*.

Where scepticism is the doubt of anything certain, cynicism is the inclination to believe that people are acting out of self-interest; to distrust their motives. And cynicism and fear are two things at root in our post-truth climate. Our felt inability to know anything (scepticism) has steered us to lead with emotion (post-truth) and, as that happens, we circle back again in cynicism, asking ourselves, 'What is the point? Will this actually make a difference?' This again fuels our scepticism that we are able to know anything. Scepticism fuels our post-truth climate leading to cynicism, which in turn fuels our post-truth climate again.

If your head is spinning, then so are those of much of society! And yet, for the Christian, we glimpse something of truth in this cycle. We weren't made to use pure emotion or pure reason detached from each other. Cynicism arises when we rightly question the value of post-truth, but there is no grounding alternative if God has been taken out of the equation. All that is left to do therefore is to circle back into post-truth, speaking even more passionately, more loudly, with extra conviction – and with mistrust in what we are saying running rife. Without an anchor for truth, the world is adrift in a sea of scepticism, cynicism and mistrust. There is no option other than to doubt others' motivations in what they say.

SO THE WORLD DOESN'T WANT TRUTH?

Taking into account our current climate, you'd be forgiven for questioning, 'Does anyone actually care about truth any more?'

Your truth, my truth, this truth, their truth, perceived truth, partial truth, distorted truth. So many 'truths' abound! Does anyone actually care about what actually *is* or *isn't* the truth any more?

The post-truth narrative would want to deceive us into thinking that people don't care about truth or that it doesn't matter. Far from it! We see from a gazillion magazines, books, internet articles, tweets and irate FB posts on post-truth that post-truth has exposed our desire *for* truth. The reason we feel let down when we are lied to is that, right in our core, we know there is a desire for truth. We feel betrayed and cheated because we feel there is a right way to live, an honest way, a truthful way. We want to be known truly, and we want to know truly. Post-truth hasn't suppressed our desire for truth; it has served to expose it. Post-truth forces us to confront lies in our continued search for a truth we can trust. Rationalism to empiricism, existentialism to post-truth and whatever will come after that: society and the human hearts that make it are searching for the *way.*

Jesus said,
'If you hold to my teaching, you are really my disciples. Then you will know the truth, and the truth will set you free.'

(John 8:31–32)

Chapter four

UNTWISTING TRUTH – CHRIST IS TRUTH

Look around you today – in work, in university, on the bus, in the street – and you will see people who don't know the way. Not just in a tourists-don't-know-where-they-are-going way, but in life. All around us, people are asking: 'What is my purpose?' 'What is the meaning of life?' 'Where do we go after we die?' 'What's the point?'

Even the disciples, Jesus' carefully selected crew, looking Truth in the eye, were asking these questions. This questioning is recorded in the Bible in John 14, where we find Jesus preparing to leave the disciples and begin his journey towards the cross. The entire purpose of his life is upon him; he is about to meet his Father in the full face of his wrath and anger. The eternal Son who has only known the truth of delightful intimacy within the Godhead is about to know the truth of God's devastating judgment upon sin. Because that's the real issue, isn't it? Not different philosophical viewpoints, not an apathy with truth. But sin. Ever since Eden, since humanity fell, sin has separated us from God. God did not abandon us in our sin and rebellion but came to rescue us, first through the sacrifices that pointed to Jesus, and then through Jesus himself coming to die for us. God sent his son Jesus to die for our sins to restore our relationship with truth once and for all. The weight of humanity's abandonment of truth in favour of lies is about to be laid upon Jesus' shoulders.

In John 14:1–4, Jesus shares the marvellous reality of his leaving. He has to leave, he has to go through death and resurrection, in order that our relationship with truth be restored and a place in his Father's house can be prepared for the disciples, and for us. He says to them, 'You know the way to the place where I am going' (14:4). Thomas then says to Jesus what they are all thinking, what many of us are thinking to this day: 'Lord, we don't know where you are going, so how can we know the way?'

Like Thomas and the other disciples, if we don't know where Jesus is going, we cannot know the way. And, as we will see later on, this is the question many in our post-truth society are currently asking: how can we know the way through the competing truth claims and many captivating calls upon our hearts? How can we know? Is there even *one* way?

WHO IS TRUTH?

Jesus confidently told his disciples that they knew the way to where he was going, but they still didn't get it. Jesus' response to Thomas is also what he says to us today (see opposite).

Jesus answered, 'I am the way and the truth and the life. No one comes to the Father except through me. If you really know me, you will know my Father as well. From now on, you do know him and have seen him.'

(John 14:6–7)

Jesus makes an outrageous claim here. He says he alone is The Way. He alone is The Truth. He alone is The Life. If we want to *know* the way, we need to *know* Jesus. If we want to know the way of salvation and life and, therefore, know the Father, only Jesus can secure, show and share him with us. Jesus uses two different words for 'know' in this phrase and the likely distinction between the usage offers further depth to his assertion: if we want knowledge *of* (*oida*) Jesus, we need knowledge *about/in* (*ginōskō*) Jesus.

We don't need to be scholars to understand that the two different words Jesus uses for 'know' are significant here. So if Greek isn't your thing, bear with me. Jesus starts by using the word *oida* when he assures the disciples they know (*oida*) the way. This kind of knowledge is knowing *of* something. It is an intellectual grasp of objective understanding.

When Thomas replies that he doesn't *oida* the way (try saying that in conversations in the future!), Jesus then says that if they really knew – *ginōskō* – him, they would know the Father too and, therefore, the way to him. This kind of knowledge is personal. Something or someone becomes known to us. It's an intimate understanding. *Ginōskō* is a much deeper knowledge than *oida*. It is also used as the 'knowing' of sexual union in the Bible. Jesus says we need both *oida* and *ginōskō*. *Ginōskō* leads to *oida* and vice versa by the Spirit (John 15). If we want knowledge *of* Jesus, we need knowledge *in* or about Jesus. Knowledge in Jesus is truth.

This is why the disciples do not yet understand. They do not know intimately, fully, the whole reason Christ came. They have called him the Messiah, they have *oida* knowledge about that now, but they don't have the personal *ginōskō* knowledge of the kind of Messiah Jesus is: they haven't yet witnessed him bleed for them in order to save them. This is also why it is possible to have knowledge of God, but not really know him. We may know many truths 'of' without knowing truth 'in'. I think of the many theologians I know who study the Scriptures day in and day out, and yet have no relationship with truth.

Ginōskō knowledge of Jesus leads to union with him in his death and resurrection. That is how we know the Father. There is so much more we could say on this, but it is of utmost importance we see that what Jesus is saying in John 14 is that he *alone* is Truth.

We are reminded later in Acts 4:12: 'there is no other name under heaven given to mankind by which we must be saved.' Jesus makes an *exclusive* truth claim. Truth isn't a matter of personal preference; it's not the pick 'n' mix approach we see much of in our society and that perhaps many of our friends have adopted. Jesus is Truth with a capital 'T'. He is not one among many. In and through Jesus the bedrock reality of the universe is revealed: God himself. The Father sends the Son in the power of the Spirit. If we know Jesus, we know truth.

WHO IS I AM?

When Jesus says 'I AM', some of you may have a few Old Testament alarm bells ringing in your head. When God reveals himself to Moses and tasks him with the little project of redeeming his people from Egypt, Moses asks God, 'Who shall I say sent me?' God replies:

> 'I AM WHO I AM. This is what you are to say to the Israelites: "I AM has sent me to you."' God also said to Moses, 'Say this to the Israelites, "The LORD, the God of your fathers – the God of Abraham, the God of Isaac and the God of Jacob – has sent me to you." This is my name forever, the name you shall call me from generation to generation.'
> (Exodus 3:14–15)

God identifies himself as 'I AM'. So, when Jesus says "I AM . . . the truth' in John 14 (and John 8), these aren't words a Jewish lad should utter if he wants to learn how to make friends with and influence Pharisees. By saying this, he is equating himself with Yahweh of Exodus 3. 'I AM' is Yahweh. He is saying he is God and, ultimately, that is why he is killed: 'Why does this fellow talk like that? He's blaspheming! Who can forgive sins but God alone?' (Mark 2:7). Jesus says he is the great 'I AM'. He alone is qualified to lead us in truth because he is Yahweh and Yahweh is Truth. He is the way, and he testifies to the truth because he is Truth; he is Yahweh. This leader testifies to truth by going to his death.

CHRIST'S TRUTHFUL TESTIMONY

Jesus knew who he was. He also knew why he was sent to earth. Jesus' claim to be Truth isn't a claim for self-serving status and power like many leaders today. Jesus does not want a platform, he knows his purpose: he comes to be pierced. 'In fact, the reason I was born and came into the world is to testify to the truth' (John 18:37).

In the face of competing truth claims and heart allegiances, we are not in so different a position to that of the early Christians. The Roman Emperor was the gods' representative on earth. Failure to worship him was seen as treason and was therefore punishable by death. There are those in the world facing a similar decision today: either exchange the truth of Christ for submission to Allah, or face certain death.

Strange though it seems, every culture sets up gods in all spheres of life, which we are expected to worship or face death by social ostracism, moral condemnation and sometimes even violence. For us, we face small 'deaths' for following Christ every day when we say we claim to know the truth and refuse to bow down before secular altars of materialism, consumerism and sexual ethics that dictate 'as long we don't harm anyone, anything goes between two consenting adults'. The people alive at the time of Jesus' death and resurrection had the same choice to make: accept or reject that Jesus is The Truth. One such person we are told about is Pontius

Pilate, a high official and leader, a magistrate of Judea. Pilate summons Jesus before him and they start chatting. Pilate is attempting to ascertain the nature of the allegations made against Jesus. We are invited to listen in on their conversation in John 18:33–38 (see opposite).

Truth matters. Like Pilate, if we walk away from truth, we walk away from Christ himself. And doing so is not a neutral act. It has consequences. For Pilate, this led to him killing Truth. This is what we do when we deny the reality of Christ in our everyday living. Sin is not a morally neutral act. We kill truth each time we sin. We live as though truth does not matter and so we sacrifice it. As author and apologist Ravi Zacharias explains, 'Pilate walks away from the greatest authority on the greatest question and committed the greatest crime at that time.'

That is what is at stake here. Not an artificial, abstract notion of the truth which is relativized beyond meaning, but Jesus himself. He either is the Way, the Truth and the Life or he isn't.

Pilate was desperate to let Jesus off the hook. He even gave people the option of choosing between releasing Jesus or the notorious criminal Barabbas in the hope they would free Jesus. When the guilty man goes free and the innocent one is sent to his death (what a gospel picture!), Pilate washes his hands of it. His fear of insurrection at a politically turbulent time far outweighed his love of truth. We too cannot sit on the fence. Any form of inaction is

Pilate then went back inside the palace, summoned Jesus and asked him, 'Are you the king of the Jews?'

'Is that your own idea,' Jesus asked, 'or did others talk to you about me?'

'Am I a Jew?' Pilate replied. 'Your own people and chief priests handed you over to me. What is it you have done?'

Jesus said, 'My kingdom is not of this world. If it were, my servants would fight to prevent my arrest by the Jewish leaders. But now my kingdom is from another place.'

'You are a king, then!' said Pilate.

Jesus answered, 'You say that I am a king. In fact, the reason I was born and came into the world is to testify to the truth. Everyone on the side of truth listens to me.'

'What is truth?' retorted Pilate.

With this he went out again.

(John 18:33–38)

action. Knowing Truth, we cannot like Pilate shrug our shoulders, say 'What is truth?' and walk away.

In Jesus, we find the truth that society is looking for. But the question remains, being human, can we know anything certainly – even truth itself? None of our knowledge is certain, despite Descartes's desire to establish it. We have seen the erosive implications of such knowledge. What we have in Christ, however, isn't certain knowledge, but *confident* knowledge. We can be confident because, as we have seen, truth is relational (as well as propositional). Our personal knowledge of Christ may be tainted by our own sin, making certainty elusive, but we can be confident because what he has revealed to us is true as a result of who he is: The God-Man. The reality is that none of us knows anything with complete certainty. Such knowledge isn't possible for us. But we can *confidently* know the one who knows all things *certainly*.

In fact,
the reason I was
born and came
into the world
is to testify
to the truth.

(John 18:37)

Chapter five

ONE TRUTH - TWO TYPES OF 'KNOWING' IT

With all the competing truth claims today, it's important we understand the kind of Truth Jesus is so that we are able to know who we believe and enjoy and how we can share him. So, what if Jesus really is, as he claims to be, 'the way and the truth and the life'? If this is true, Jesus shows that truth is a person. Truth is Jesus Christ. Truth is the God–Man. And he has made truth known to us through his life, death and resurrection. Let's look more deeply at this.

WHAT DOES JESUS MEAN WHEN HE SAYS HE IS THE TRUTH?

1 Objective truth (oida)

In John 14, after Jesus responds to Thomas' question with some of the most explosive words in history, Philip then pipes up. He, too, doesn't quite understand how Jesus can show them the Father. Philip says, 'Lord, show us the Father and that will be enough for us' (14:8).

Jesus is not quite enough for them. After all they have seen, heard and tasted while they have been with Jesus, they still do not recognize from whom he has come and why. This is what we are tempted to lose sight of in our historical moment. We, like the disciples, are tempted to believe that perhaps Jesus isn't quite enough. It cannot be that simple. Surely we need something more? Show us truth definitively, then we will believe! Open the skies, tell us this is truth, 'show us the Father'.

And he does (see opposite).

Jesus shares the authority of the Father, who is living in him, through his words and his works: all the time he has spent with the disciples, the care, the wise words, the words of comfort, the words of prophecy, the powerful words that have raised friends from the dead, calmed storms and turned water into wine. Jesus says we know he is the Truth through what he has said and what he has done. The Father has shown us definitive truth in Jesus by the Spirit. And the greatest thing, his greatest work, was going to the cross for sinners like you and me. As the God–Man he has the power to say, 'Friend, your sins are forgiven' (Luke 5:20). This is Truth that does not change with the winds of political mood or personal preference. He is someone we can anchor our lives to.

Jesus is objective, external Truth. The truth of his life has witnesses. He is declarative and propositional Truth. He can be tested. Jesus demonstrates the truth of his identity through his life and death

Jesus answered: 'Don't you know me, Philip, even after I have been among you such a long time? Anyone who has seen me has seen the Father. How can you say, "Show us the Father"? Don't you believe that I am in the Father, and that the Father is in me? The words I say to you I do not speak on my own authority. Rather, it is the Father, living in me, who is doing his work. Believe me when I say that I am in the Father and the Father is in me; or at least believe on the evidence of the works themselves. Very truly I tell you, whoever believes in me will do the works I have been doing, and they will do even greater things than these, because I am going to the Father. And I will do whatever you ask in my name, so that the Father may be glorified in the Son. You may ask me for anything in my name, and I will do it.'

(John 14:9–14)

and resurrection as recorded in the Bible. This isn't a truth claim made drinking into the night in someone's back garden. This is recorded in history. We are not left guessing, 'but how can we know you are the way?', as Thomas asked. Jesus is The Public Truth claim. His whole being carries ultimate authority from the Father himself and, as John goes on to share, the work and presence of the power of the Spirit in chapter 15. The objective truth of Jesus gives us confidence in knowing that Truth is true. We cannot mess with the words and works of Jesus. They happened in space-time history and there is exceptional historical attestation to their veracity. It is patently false, lies and error to say that there are many ways to know God. There is only one. Truth himself.

What Jesus shows us is that facts matter. It is not like one of Joe Dator's cartoons with the words, 'I'm sorry, Jeannie, your answer was correct, but Kevin shouted his incorrect answer over yours so he gets the points.' It's more like the observation of influential twentieth-century historian Timothy Snyder in *On Tyranny*: 'to abandon facts is to abandon freedom'. And none more so than when it comes to Jesus. Objective truth in Christ corrects the false move of post-truth where we have let emotions and feelings have the final word. Jesus shows us that the external *words* and *works* of his life count. We need objectivity: we need 'knowledge of' (*oida*).

2 Subjective truth (ginōskō)

But we aren't called to have mere objective truth. Jesus is Truth with flesh on. This kind of knowledge walks. Truth is not just an 'out there' declaration of truth, one that is open to public scrutiny and examination. Jesus shows us that truth is also necessarily personal (*ginōskō*). He demonstrates that the external words and works of his life count as the *eternal Word takes on flesh so that we can know him*. As theologian Steven Garber wrote in *Visions of Vocation*: 'As humans we have to see words made flesh to understand them.' This means we can have a relationship with the Father through Jesus! We can have a relationship with God himself.

In John 14:13–14 Jesus says that through faith in him we are able to talk to him. We can pray to him in his name, *and* he will listen, *and* he will answer because he wants to glorify the Father. This is the best kind of personal truth. Jesus is other-person-centred Truth. We are personally brought into Jesus' desire to glorify the Father. Jesus answers our prayers so that the Father can be glorified in him. And the way he does this, the way he restores our relationship with truth, is through his death on a cross. Not apple experiments, not reductionist theory, but in dying for the sins that keep us from knowing the truth personally. As writer and philosopher George Steiner puts it in *No Passion Spent*: 'The fatal tree of Adam and Eve will reappear as the wood of the Cross.'

We ultimately see that Christ is Truth on the cross. Through God we see the declarative standards of holy, sinless living before him in the law, but we also see the personal fulfilment of these in Jesus himself as the God-Man. A medieval Archbishop of Canterbury, Anselm, wrote that humans *should* repay the debt of sin, but only

God *could*. John Stott, the late church leader and author, when paraphrasing Anselm in *The Cross of Christ* said this: 'Jesus is therefore the only Saviour since he is the only person in whom the "should" and the "could" are united, being himself both God and man.' In Jesus, we see not only divinity and humanity perfectly coexisting but also objective and subjective understanding.

BOTH/AND NOT EITHER/OR

The quests and quibbles for truth we followed the philosophers through earlier are ultimately resolved in Christ. The eternal reason of God has taken on flesh and walked among us. Is truth then external, internal, objective, subjective? It is all in Christ. It is the declarative statements and actual events of his words and works, but they are centred in his person. Truth is personal because Jesus is. He has walked among us. He achieved for us what we could not: eternal life in relationship with God. This means that truth is no less than objective, it is so much more. It is also no less than subjective, it is so much more.

Come,
see a man
who told me
everything
I ever did.
Could this be
the Messiah?

(John 4:29)

Chapter six

TRUTH IS PERSONAL - RELATIONAL TRUTH

Truth does not come to us a in a vacuum. It is textured. It is objective, yes: it can be tested, supported by facts. And yet, it is intrinsically personal. This is the reason why we feel betrayed when we are misled, and why there are personal repercussions, so much opinion and pain, littering our post-truth and uncertain world.

We feel let down by politicians, by experts, by social media. We do not think people want to serve us with the truth. All they want to do is to manipulate truth to serve themselves. I'm sure we can all remember the Brexit slogans from not so long ago. 'Let's give our NHS the £350 million the EU takes every week,' politicians told our public. But when the numbers had been crunched and a more accurate estimation was produced, Boris Johnson and Iain Duncan Smith were very quick to deny this claim. Statements such as this prompt us to question: how can we recognize when someone is telling us the truth? People promise much and deliver little. As we have seen, our nation has become weary of experts, from social media sites such as Facebook to even our democracy being challenged, with *The Guardian* reporting that a parliamentary committee is expected to say: 'Democracy is at risk unless the government and regulators take urgent action to combat a growing crisis of data manipulation, disinformation and so-called fake news.'

We experience cynicism, our lack of trust in truth, because these sources of truth have let us down. We feel betrayed because, as the Bible asserts, truth is personal.

TRUTH RELATES TO US

If truth is personal, it is also *relational*. If someone lies, they lie to *us*. If someone confronts our lies with the truth, we have to admit our deception. This is a massive stumbling block for many in society: to accept that Jesus is the Truth, we need to admit that lies, sin, have entered our hearts, repent of them and turn back to him. To say Jesus is the Truth, we have to admit we have denied this, that we have lied.

Ever since that fateful garden day, we have been unable to see truth for what it is: true! The remedy isn't to change our post-truth culture, because culture isn't the problem. Culture is an expression of human values, and if those values are the product of fallen human hearts we should expect the culture they produce to be fallen: warped, twisted and perverted in all sorts of ways. For some it is the stumbling block of having to admit we are sinners that keeps us separated from truth. A bit like that scene from *A Few Good Men*: 'You want the truth? You can't handle the truth!'

This inability to face up to the truth was brought to life for me recently as I was wandering through the art museum in Vienna. Stumbling upon an amazing painting of a woman by one of Austria's finest artists, Klimt, I read her name: Nuda Veritas – *Naked Truth*. She stands tall in all her red-headed, naked simplicity. But she is holding something. She has a mirror in her hand and it is facing outwards, to you, to me. The museum describes her as not 'beautiful or idealized'. She just is. The shock at truth being a naked woman was palpable when it first went on display! People want to look away. That is pretty much what Klimt was trying to communicate. Above her are the words, written in German: 'If you can't please everybody with your deeds and your art, please only a few'. A serpent of envy creeps towards her from the perspective of the viewer. It is as though Klimt is saying, 'You can't handle what you most want. You envy that which you despise.' We can often be repulsed by someone who is confident in the truth because, deep down, it is what we really long to know ourselves.

WE KNOW THE WAY, BUT DO WE WANT TO FOLLOW?

As truth is relational, it will have implications in our own lives: to turn from sin, to turn towards truth. Sometimes, therefore, we can know Truth, but we don't really want to follow. We know he has called us to deny ourselves, take up our crosses and follow him (Matthew 16:24), but do we want to?

When someone says to us, 'You can't possibly be so naïve as to believe there is only one Truth, can you?', do we begin to doubt because *we do not know* the way, or because *we do not want to* incur the cost of following Truth? We know the way of Truth, but we do not want to walk in him because Jesus looks silly and unsophisticated to a society that sometimes feels like it's going in a different direction. Jesus calls us to listen to and follow truth in him: 'Everyone on the side of truth listens to me' (John 18:37).

The truth we all want, whoever we are, whether we know him or not, is found in him alone. Rather than this being a restrictive option that narrows down our experience of truth in life, he instead liberates us from sin in order to enjoy truth where he truly is. We will not enjoy the fullness of this in this life. That is why he comforts the disciples by saying he is preparing a room for them in his Father's house, *with him*. On that day, when Jesus returns, we will see him face to face. For now, as Paul reminds us, we see through a mirror dimly. Does this mean we will only see partial truth now? In some ways, yes. There is much we do not know, but what we need to know for salvation has been given to us in Jesus.

This means that if we deny truth in Christ, we deny our salvation. Christ alone is the Truthful Leader who can lead us to intimate truth of himself, if we let him. Who will you follow? Will you follow Christ knowing you belong to him as you do and you already belong to him by faith through grace? This does not close down questioning for us. It closes down intentional ignorance. We need to ask questions. We need to seek answers. And we need to keep doing this throughout our Christian lives. God loves a sincere heart in search of truth. But the challenge for all of us is to listen to truth and not retreat into scepticism whenever truth presents something personally unpalatable to us.

BUT IS HE GOOD?

Christ's words leave little wiggle room. In the same way that we can doubt the motive of a leader telling us the best thing for our country, or a social-media mogul telling us that facemasks really will work, we can often find ourselves doubting the trustworthiness of Christ – especially when it leads to us denying ourselves or looking silly. We often do not want to follow the truth in the way of Christ because we doubt that he is really good.

We all too easily understand his objective truth value: he has power and authority to say and do all things. But we are slow to believe that power can be wielded for our good. Our post-truth context has shown us the consequences of abuse of power, and so we are slow to trust because we believe others do not have our best interests at heart. They have their own and they want to manipulate us to suit their own ends and needs. We are slow to follow truth because we doubt truth can be good for us. Here lies the heart of our personal resistance when we meet Christ as Truth for the first time, and as we continue to follow him. Is he really good? We often measure goodness by safety. Truth is good if it is safe and therefore makes little demands on me. It doesn't call me to be distinctive when faced with multiple truth claims, for example. Thankfully, we are not alone in wanting Jesus to be safe. In C. S. Lewis's *The Lion, the Witch and the Wardrobe*, Lucy asks this very same question of Mr Beaver:

> 'Aslan is a lion – the Lion, the great Lion.'
>
> 'Ooh,' said Susan. 'I'd thought he was a man. Is he – quite safe? I shall feel rather nervous about meeting a lion.'
>
> 'Safe?' said Mr Beaver. 'Who said anything about safe? 'Course he isn't safe. But he's good. He's the King, I tell you.'

Following Jesus is one the least safe things we could ever do. He turns lives upside down and inside out. He transforms hearts. But in this we know he is good: he comes for us through the cross so that we can have life in him and with him. He is the King, I tell you.

Perhaps, though, there is a little voice in the back of your head wondering, 'Isn't all this stuff about Jesus just another post-truth claim? An outright lie that sounds good so people go for it?' With confidence we can say Jesus is Truth because he entered the broken system and revealed a better way. He is the ultimate outsider and anti-establishment voice. His isn't a private truth claim brokered in the back corridors to halls of power to maximize personal gain, but an open, public truth claim that he backed up with his own life, death and resurrection. He is there to be tested, scrutinized and investigated. Yet, he is also the ultimate insider. Instead of saying, 'Washington doesn't work', we can say, 'The Word works', because he knows me. He is a human being. He knows my failings, desires and longings. He is able to identify with me in every weakness and aspect, apart from sin.

And that is why we can trust in him.

By this everyone will know that you are my disciples, if you love one another.

(John 13:35)

Chapter seven

TRUTH DIVIDES - DIVERSITY AND UNITY

Truth comes with flesh on, so the way we experience truth is very much tailored by who is saying it. Could it be that our own distrust of the Jesus story comes from a sense of betrayal from the church on a corporate and personal level?

Many of us distrust the church. We aren't short of reasons to do so. We read of sex scandals and leadership misconduct in the USA and in the UK with surprising regularity. It is heart-breaking. And for those of us who have been profoundly influenced by their ministries, the pain goes deeper still. It leaves us wondering if it is possible to live a good life. Is the Christian life just too hard to keep going until the end? When the 'best' struggle, it makes us question whether we will be able to go the distance. In the space of two months, the characters of three of my personal heroes were called into question. These are men and women who were instrumental in my coming to know the Lord in the first place! It hurt. My cynicism was profound. It left me wondering if there were any trustworthy Christians left. Aren't we all as bad as one another? Whom can I trust with my weary heart?

More personally devastating, perhaps you've been abused in the worst possible ways by those in authority, those you loved and respected. Perhaps no-one else sees them, but the wounds remain raw. A sermon on Sunday or even well-meaning, seemingly harmless statements from friends: 'Trust me!' Ha. Yeah. Sure. Our scars tell the stories of those we have trusted in the past. We have levelled-up since then. We know better than to be so naïve as to trust someone, especially those who seem the most trustworthy.

On a smaller scale in church life, it could even be the belittling and damaging 'you're wrong, I'm right' subtext undergirding some of our conversations that can cause pain and frustration. Our personal pain filters the way we view Jesus. All these experiences colour the way we view truth. And rightly so! I remember author and friend Mark Meynell speaking of church as a 'heavenly outpost'. Wow! A place where the light and life of Christ dwells, where we see the loving kindness of our God in and through others by his Spirit. But when we are met with pain in a place where we seek healing, it is no wonder we leave with distrust in our hearts. The church is meant to reflect the character of God. But sometimes the god we see reflected back at us is that of the world, of fallen hearts, not the God of truth, love and grace.

This further demonstrates the personal dimension to truth. It has both damaging and healing effects. Disintegration of truth leads to disintegration of trust. As the church, or religion on a broader scale, has so often let us down, so often been hurtful or hypocritical in its bold truth claims, our society has increasingly sought to smooth everything over and soothe the hurt through harmonization.

LIVE YOUR BEST LIFE

In fear of pushing our truth on others to hurtful effects, we are now told to 'live your best life'. You can decide whatever that is; it's whatever is most true to *you*. And it's no wonder, because though on an individual level we are all crying out for the truth, at the same time society wants to harmonize difference.

I recently spent a sweaty half hour trekking up to a piece of art called the *Garden of Philosophy* on Gellért Hill in Budapest. It is a beautiful location with sweeping panoramic views of the Danube basin. The sculptures in this garden express society's motivation towards harmony. Nándor Wagner created this piece (also placed in Japan and the USA) in 1997 in an effort to promote mutual understanding between the main world religions. Statues of Akhenaten, Abraham, Jesus, Lao Tse and Buddha all circle around an orb presenting their commonality. It communicates the need to understand one another, but it goes even further than that. In fact, the way it has been constructed seems to say that, at heart, all these religions believe the same thing: following Jesus is similar to channelling the inner peace of Buddha, which is also similar to worshipping Allah, which is not so different from the monotheism imposed by Akhenaten. All these religions tap into that same human desire to worship. They are just different expressions of it. Isn't this what we are also tempted to believe?

This *Garden of Philosophy* is a microcosm of what we are seeing in society today. This is what society communicates. In the face of religious violence, political turbulence and LGBTQIA questions, among others, we cannot claim that any one of us knows truth. To do so collapses our harmony. It flies in the face of tolerance. It is an act of violence.

Harmonizing truth claims is the only solution society provides us with when it's faced with multiple options. A lack of harmony, disagreement, is an expression of a lack of love, and that is dangerous and unpredictable. Difference, therefore, needs to be dialled down. We feel the very same impulse as Christians for the very same reason. We know truth matters, but we fear asserting truth claims in case we alienate others. So, for many of us, we too dial down the difference. For others, in fear of losing the 'truth' through this watered-down homogeny, we assert it even more forcefully.

A DIVIDED TRUTH?

In many ways, the harmony society desires should be found *within* the church, a people fully united in their love of God. Paul, in his first letter to the Corinthians, urged:

> I appeal to you, brothers and sisters, in the name of our Lord Jesus Christ, that all of you agree with one another in what you say and that there be no divisions among you, but that you be perfectly united in mind and thought.
>
> (1 Corinthians 1:10)

And again in his letter to the Colossians:

> Bear with each other and forgive one another if any of you has a grievance against someone. Forgive as the Lord forgave you. And over all these virtues put on love, which binds them all together in perfect unity.
>
> (Colossians 3:13–14)

Where the church or churches in a particular area join together in unity, amazing things happen as communities see a glimpse of God's heart. For example, where churches have united to serve the homeless or come together to support the mission and faith of CUs within universities. It is marvellous to behold. Many, however, often do not see this. Instead they see churches as disgruntled groups of people who cannot get along. I'm sure if we're honest, there are times when we see people in other church denominations or expressions and simply can't identify with their 'truth' or the way they are sharing it. The problem is that garden post-truth suspicion has also seeped into the way we view ourselves as Christians, into what we accept as 'truth' from our church leaders and how we try to share this inherently 'personned' truth with others.

OUR CHURCH CULTURES

The way we understand the truth as Christians inherently shapes our churches and the cultures they portray to ourselves and others. If we were to make a sweeping generalization as to how truth has been 'known' and 'portrayed' by the church today, we could crudely split our churches into two key camps: charismatics and conservatives. This distinction is not meant to invoke tribalism but, as we look through these broad categorizations, it doesn't take long to see that the way we view truth is fundamentally wedded to the life and character of our churches. Truth forms and fuels the way we preach, teach and train, worship, sing, pray and fellowship. Personality and culture also have a lot to do with this, but the primary way we view the truth will be the primary way we *practise* it. While you may identify with features from both these examples, how we practise truth is the prevailing means by which we can identify the way we view truth. It is this truth that we then portray to the outside world.

Conservative

If you have ever visited one of these churches, or you've been blessed to belong to one, you'll know very quickly that, upon arriving on a Sunday, the whole service focuses on the preached Word of God, the Bible. Some of the best corporate singing I've ever enjoyed has been in these contexts, singing together as an 'us' and a 'we' about God. A young woman I know called Gloria, who belongs to a charismatic church, shared with me her experience of checking out the conservative church many of her university friends attended:

> As I entered, I was given a sermon outline by someone on the door and told to sit near the front. After singing a couple of songs, the speaker welcomed us and shared about the sermon series the church would be spending the next month on. A passage was read out and then the speaker took us through verse by verse, teasing things out that I'd never seen or heard before. We sang another couple of songs and I noticed that most people stood quite still, not expressing much emotion, but they did try to make eye contact with me and others as we sang about 'our' hope in Jesus. At the end, I filled in a card, the speaker came over to say hello and informed me about home groups and the ways I could serve in the church. Everyone else was talking in groups, so I slipped out, marvelling at all I'd heard from the Scriptures.

Charismatic

If you've ever visited a charismatic church, or you've been blessed to belong to one, the starkest difference between this and Gloria's experience above is perhaps the amount of time spent singing to God with one another. Often a good half an hour is devoted to worship. Another difference may be the snacks. Stereotypically, you may be offered a barista-quality coffee and pastries before you take your seat. The sermon will often be thematic: you may have a talk on identity rather than on the book of John, for example. But that doesn't mean the Bible won't be included! Often, in these theological settings, practical authority may lean towards the role of the Spirit at work in individuals. After the sermon, there will often be an extended time of prayer ministry. Joe, who belongs to a conservative church, having heard wonderful things about what God had been doing in his local charismatic church, decided to visit. Here are his thoughts:

> I was 500 yards from the front door, and I was already being greeted by broad smiles and hellos. Upon arriving I received multiple warm handshakes, followed by an enthusiastic encouragement to grab my coffee and take it into the meeting room with me. A guy introduced himself and asked whether it was my first visit, before sitting down next to me, even taking my number at the end and texting me to see how I was doing later that day. We worshipped and then the speaker spoke on the topic of praise, how we can develop lives centred on thankfulness before God. The speaker went to lots of different places in the Bible to make the point, and then encouraged us to pray for friends and family who may be weighed down by life at the moment. We were invited to receive prayer for ourselves as we were encouraged to receive the Spirit's work in our daily lives. We were then encouraged to bring our friends to church and along to a seeker meeting during the week. I left feeling known and encouraged.

Once again, these distinctions are crude and rough. Charismatics would say they *are* committed to the Scriptures, and there *are* warm conservative churches! But for anyone walking into church or into a different church setting from the one you're usually used to (and I highly recommend it!), you'll see that the way we understand truth deeply affects the way we express it. Working in an interdenominational setting for the past eight years that celebrates both of these cultures, as well as coming from a diverse church background myself, this is where the direction, content and place of truth (though, of course, ultimate authority for both is in the Bible) can often be seated in the conservative/charismatic divide (see Table 1).

Table 1

	Conservative	*Charismatic*
Direction of truth	outward/proclamational	inward/pastoral
Content of truth	'You need to repent'	'I need to repent'
Place of truth	mind	heart

And, as cultural beings, we can see our post-truth, present-day mindset creeping into the way we live out this truth, often leading to cynicism and syncretism (adapting to cultural norms; see Table 2 on page 64).

The sceptical air we breathe encourages us to dislocate truth in either objective or subjective ways, mainly depending upon which side of the chart we identify with most. We can see that our

Table 2

	Conservative	*Charismatic*
Post-truth	emphasizes God's objective truth as the cure	emphasizes God's personal care as the cure
Cynicism	'I don't trust that you know enough in order to speak into my life'	'I don't trust that you really know me in order to pastor me well'
Syncretism	'I'll try harder!' (works)	What's the use?'(conformation)

conservative positions can lead us to view truth as primarily external, the work of the Scriptures, and our charismatic positions can lead us to view truth as primarily internal, the work of the Spirit. This means that when we consider our post-truth climate, we will have different ways of addressing it.

WHAT OUR CHURCH CULTURES SAY TO OUR UNCERTAIN WORLD

The conservative will typically call upon God's objective truth as a corrective to post-truth's preference to trust personal belief over that of the 'expert'. For example, the more conservative among us may say, 'Did you know that God is unchanging and his word is perfect? He knows this post-truth situation better than anyone else. In fact, the Bible is full of the ways he declares his knowledge and wisdom above that of people. His truth doesn't manipulate. We can stand on his unshakeable, eternal truth.'

The more charismatic sides of our church culture, on the other hand, will typically call upon a different kind of personal care as the corrective to post-truth's personal preferences. For example, the charismatic may well respond to the person on the bus who says they listen to people who aren't dry, people who believe what they are saying, with: 'Did you know that God is the only one who really *knows* you? He knows how many hairs there are on your head. He knows you better than you know yourself.'

In addressing our post-truth, 'your truth, my truth, what is truth?' age, the conservative will typically want to offer a different kind of objective truth, whereas the charismatic will typically want to offer a different kind of personal care.

CYNICISM IN OUR CHURCH CULTURES

In the same way that our post-truth age creeps into our church culture, the cynicism inherent in it affects our church culture too. It can often be seen to have two different outworkings in church life: conservatives will typically try harder at applying themselves, even if it's devoid of heart engagement, while charismatics may feel overwhelmed and typically question the point in continuing, even though they may hold on to some aspect of belief. Conservatives, prizing head knowledge of the Scriptures, may begin to distrust and withdraw from anyone who doesn't know 'their stuff'. Charismatics, prizing heart knowledge, may come to distrust anyone who doesn't seem to care about them personally.

This is how the post-truth cycle turns in church. It's important we see how this works in our own hearts and cultures if we are to:

> Do everything without grumbling or arguing, so that you may become blameless and pure, 'children of God without fault in a warped and crooked generation.' Then you will shine among them like stars in the sky as you hold firmly to the word of life.
>
> (Philippians 2:14–16)

Not only does it help us to be better witnesses, as we will see later, but it will also increase our love for one another as we choose not to argue or grumble over our differences, but rejoice in them. There is only one basis for biblical diversity in unity. And this basis increases our depth of unity in Christ as we refuse to settle for superficial unity that doesn't consider biblical difference.

DIVERSITY IN THE TRINITY

Christ reveals diversity in unity by revealing the Trinity. As we have glimpsed throughout John's Gospel, we see the work of this tremendous Trinity securing salvation for God's people. The Father is in the Son (John 14:10), the Son is in the Father and they send the Holy Spirit (John 14:16–17). They are one God in three divine persons. There is unity in their diversity. They are distinct but not separate, united in their eternal, co-equal and divine essence. Within the Trinity, we find a real solution to society's desire for unity in diversity. It does not mean we have to say everything is acceptable, but in love we can disagree because our unity isn't based on agreement of secondary issues (like women preaching or the role of charismatic gifts), but in knowing and being found in Truth himself. In Ephesians 2:18, Paul encourages us that 'through [Christ] we both have access to the Father by one Spirit'. There is now neither Jew nor Gentile, slave nor free, man nor woman, conservative nor charismatic. We are all one in Christ through the Spirit who unites us and gives us access to the Father. Our unity is based on this important uniting truth in our diversity.

Therefore
    I am now going
    to allure her;
I will lead her
    into the
    wilderness
and speak
    tenderly to her.

(Hosea 2:14)

Chapter eight

TASTING TRUTH 1 - LISTENING TO THE TRUTH

'Knowledge is knowing that a tomato is a fruit; wisdom is not putting it in a fruit salad.' If you've been on this planet for more than a minute, you've probably heard this famous quote from Miles Kingston. It wasn't until my recent trip to Venice, however, that the sentiment of Kingston's knowledge and wisdom distinction was made all the more real to me.

'Go and have gelato!' they said. 'You'll love it!' they said. So I did.

Moments into my trip, I found myself in a quaint little ice-cream-cum-coffee shop, eyeballing around twenty different varieties of ice cream. You know how you can usually tell the flavour by the picture on the card? Yellow ice cream generally has a picture of a lemon on it, pink, a picture of a strawberry. Easy and accessible for an international audience! As I took my time gazing upon all these delicious treats, a bright blue ice cream with a picture of a Smurf on top caught my eye. I was raised on the Smurfs. I love them! So I ordered.

The waiter looked perplexed. He asked me again if I really wanted to choose that one. Of course, I did! When I ate it, it tasted like blueberries and I felt great.

I then went to Rome not long afterwards and made a point of finding this ice cream. Once more the waiter asked me, 'Are you sure, *bella*?'

'*Si!*' I replied. 'I was asked this question before.'

'I'm not surprised,' he said, before tentatively adding, 'you do know it's Viagra, don't you?'

I didn't know whether to laugh or to cry. Knowledge is knowing the Italians put Viagra in their ice cream; wisdom is not eating it! How do we *know* truth and apply it *wisely*?

THE WAY OF THE WISE

Before we answer this question, it is important to note what it means to be wise: truly wise, not just the wisdom that steers us clear of dodgy ice cream! Asserting truth does not make us wise; living in truth does. Wisdom is Truth applied: Christ lived out.

One of my favourite verses in the Bible is from the book of Proverbs: 'Go to the ant, you sluggard; consider its ways and be wise!' (Proverbs 6:6). Here we are given a biblical mandate to look at something outside the Scriptures in order to gain wisdom. We can see wisdom in creation and it is as we consider the ways of something that we can be made wise. But we can also be made foolish. Considering the ways of reality TV, for example, could lead either to wisdom or to folly. This is not to say that it's in and of itself *unwise* and not to be watched, but we are, with a discerning spirit, to weigh what messages in it are truthful or harmful and test what we take on and live out accordingly. Perhaps the only way *isn't* Essex?

As we see how the ant applies itself to work, we learn. The lazy person is given wisdom as the truth of the little ant going about its business moving, rolling and building so industriously speaks to us. Humans are told by God we can grow wise through something as small as an ant. Wisdom, then, isn't something we are zapped with when we come to Christ and receive him. It is hard work. Often slow. It means considering the way of things, using biblical lenses. So much more could be said on this, but we are going to look at how we can be wise *in* Christ.

We have seen that Christ is Truth; he is the only way and he upholds the tension between 'knowledge of' (objective) and 'knowledge in/about' (subjective) in the way we know. As we have also seen, the ultimate difference truth makes to our lives is the fact that we are saved. We can now know the Father in Christ and have access to him. In Christ we are liberated from the bondage of sin to know truth. But what does this mean for us in our day-to-day living? It is all too easy to assert truth in Christ, and not have any idea how he makes any practical difference to our lives. We will look at two different areas of our lives, what this means for us and what it means as we relate to others in community. First, we are called to *listen* to the truth.

Belonging leads to listening

Returning to the Gospel of John, Jesus' words to Pilate are startling: 'those who belong to truth listen to my voice' (John 18:37, The Berean Study Bible). Jesus says what we belong to, we listen to: those who belong to Truth listen to Truth himself. The thing is, we are always listening to something and it isn't always Jesus.

Social media, for example, feeds us lies about what it looks like to belong to the truth every single day. How often do we find ourselves scrolling down feeds of new homes, jobs, clean-eating, Pilates, the lifestyles of the rich and the famous, getting the perfect body or the perfect puppy (if you're me!)? We are bombarded by relentless voices calling on us to belong to them. This is the standard of truth we silently listen to in those minutes before falling asleep, and they are the first calls to truth we are greeted with in the morning. And we absorb these subtle messages that tell us if our lives are less than this, we don't belong.

But social media feeds and the rest of the noise that assails us are not the source of our true confidence and hope. And we know it.

Listening leads to peace (or not!)

Whether it's social media, newspapers, our friends, our work colleagues – what we listen to we think about, whether consciously or subconsciously. Paul the apostle knew this as he warned the church in Philippi:

> whatever is true, whatever is noble, whatever is right, whatever is pure, whatever is lovely, whatever is admirable – if anything is excellent or praiseworthy – think about such things. Whatever you have learned or received or heard from me, or seen in me – put it into practice. And the God of peace will be with you.
> (Philippians 4:8–9)

I've been listening to the podcast *Criminal* recently. You may have come across it. Each week they focus on different cold cases of criminal events or psychological phenomena. I was listening to one about the mind of criminals and how surprised they were in the course of their research to find that the majority of people in an educated classroom environment had entertained specific thoughts about killing someone. It was an insightful episode considering human nature – lots of great stuff in there to ponder and chew over. But it was later that night while I was doing the washing up that I found myself wondering, 'How would I kill someone?' What I'd been listening to, a podcast on murder, was trying to conform my thinking into that of a murderer. Don't worry, I have zero criminal intent.

Or do I? Jesus addresses our thought-life in his sermon on the mount in Matthew 5. He starts by reciting the law regarding murder: do not murder, those who murder will be judged, and then in a remarkable turn of events, he goes as far as to say:

> But I say to you that everyone who is angry with his brother will be liable to judgment; whoever insults his brother will be liable to the council; and whoever says, 'You fool!' will be liable to the hell of fire.
> (Matthew 5:22, ESV)

We can kill others without having killed them and, in so doing, kill ourselves. This scripture goes to the heart of *motive*. Thankfully, my fleeting thought after listening to *Criminal* wasn't rooted in anger and rage, and I swiped it away as quickly as I would a WhatsApp notification. But it goes to show that what we listen to, and how we think upon what we listen to and respond to it, is the difference between having the peace of God or being liable to the fire of hell. Hatred, even if it isn't acted upon, is just as lethal as an act of hatred. Why is this the case? Surely it's a little unfair? It's because what we listen to, as in what we take in and let control our thoughts and change our hearts, indicates who we belong to. As we belong to the truth, let's keep on encouraging one another to ask for forgiveness from God when what we listen to leads us into lies, rather than into 'whatever is true'.

Listening leads to wisdom

But surely to hear only what is 'noble and true' would be to disengage from society entirely? We are called to be in the world but not of it (John 17:16). How do we listen to truth by filling our minds with what is true, pure and lovely while watching *Love Island* and indulging in the regular cheeky Netflix binge? If we listen to what we belong to, does that mean we should stop doing these things and others altogether?

For some of us, the answer could very well be yes. If by listening to these voices we lose our confidence in truth, then it could be time for a break. Sadly, we often only notice this when it's too late. Applying truth to these areas of our lives may mean asking ourselves particular questions as we watch things. For example: What am I being told is good and desirable here? Why? What would Truth say about this? What is the glimpse of truth that may be twisted in what I'm watching?

What we listen to affects us profoundly. We like to think there is a disconnect between our heads and our hearts, that we can just listen to things because we want to or because others do without it affecting them. But, as we've seen from Philippians, what we think about and focus on will either keep us close to the God of peace or it won't. Our consciences are usually quick to point this out. The world will laugh at us for this: 'Are you afraid something you hear may offend your fragile sensibilities? Poor naïve little Christian! Always denying yourself.' This is where wisdom walks in. In the words of the philosopher Montaigne, 'a wise man sees as much as he ought, not as much as he can'.

We are normal people (well, most of us) who aren't usually afraid to engage with 'worldly' things, but truth tells how we *ought* to engage, not how much we can. If you don't need a break from Instagram or other social media platforms, why not say to yourself before you open the app, 'Be discerning. What are the lies? Where is the truth?' And remember, it is by focusing on *truth* that we can discern lies: whose words are we actively listening to and allowing to shape our belonging? Even those well-framed pictures of others reading the Bible in a moment of tranquillity with an artisan coffee have been placed for optimum effect. Those moments rarely exist and, if they do, let's celebrate them with others, but let's not be lured into thinking that that is the model and prime way we show our godliness. When you look at someone's perfectly symmetrical make-up, are you listening to the lie 'you should look like this', or to the truth that you are 'fearfully and wonderfully made' (Psalm 139:14)? When you look at your friend's new sports car, are you listening to the lie 'I *need* that', or the truth that 'life does not consist in an abundance of possessions' (Luke 12:15)? When you look at a photo of the perfect engagement as you settle down for another night of Netflix and chill (very much literally, very much alone), do you listen to the lie 'I'm missing out, God's never going to give me what I want', or to the truth, trusting God to give you not what you want, but what you *need*, resting in him, believing Truth when he says, 'Do not worry about tomorrow' (Matthew 6:25–34)? Listening to truth doesn't mean we should abandon culture, but rather learn to analyse it critically.

A TENDER TRUTH

We listen to truth by listening to Jesus. As the Spirit of Truth presses his truth into our hearts, the external words and work of Jesus are made personal to us and we see the dynamic of listening to truth at play. When we read God's words in the Bible, we listen to him. In doing so, the Spirit applies Christ to our hearts. We are filled with Christ's Spirit as we listen to him and as we walk in him. As Paul says, 'What we have received is not the spirit of the world, but the Spirit who is from God, so that we may understand what God has freely given us' (1 Corinthians 2:12).

And this truth isn't timid or conditional or hard to find. God wants to woo us when we want to whore ourselves out to other lovers. This is one of the most beautiful and outrageous parts of the book of Hosea. Having listed all the indictments against Israel, God says, '*therefore*, I will allure her into the desert and speak tenderly to her' (Hosea 2:14, emphasis added). It is because we are weak and we sin by listening to other attractive voices and tempting offers that God says he will speak to us tenderly. In the desert. Perhaps you know precisely what is calling your heart away from Christ at the moment. It could be niggling doubts over truth claims, or loves you don't think will help you to walk in truth. Whatever it is, God still and always will want to woo you.

I was at an annual leadership conference one year sitting next to a dear friend. We were crammed in side by side so as many people as possible could be seated on those awful white plastic chairs. It wasn't very comfortable. So I was quite surprised when, at the end of the meeting, my friend just leant forward, buried her face in her hands and refused to look up. Most people were in the process of getting up, getting out, trying as they might to shake off the 'numb-bum' effect. My friend, however, was not going anywhere. Her few words were lost in mumbling as the music drowned out any discernible speech. I knelt beside her, trying to get as close to her face as possible. It remained hidden in her hands as the odd tearful shudder exercised her deep pain.

'What's troubling your heart?' I asked quietly.

Quieter still and with deep emotion she whispered, 'I don't think I believe.'

'OK,' I replied.

She proceeded to give reasons why she didn't think God existed any more. She then said, wonderfully revealingly, 'I don't think he loves me.'

Isn't this what lies at the heart of most of our profound doubts? We tend to wrap up our heartache with presentable intellectual packaging. We are afraid that if we admit our need for love, he may not actually want to meet us in those deep, cavernous recesses of our hurting and weary hearts. All sorts of things call us away from walking in the truth, but what if it is also our fear of saying, 'I want the Truth to love me' and, 'I'm afraid he might not if I admit it, not after what I've done, tasted and seen'?

He wants to speak tenderly to you and remind you of his goodness, presence, intimacy and loving kindness. Truth has not left you alone. Perhaps he has taken you into a desert so that he can meet you there. Are you listening?

If we claim to
be without sin,
we deceive
ourselves and
the truth is
not in us.

(1 John 1:8)

Chapter nine

We are not only called to listen to Truth and know it in our minds, we are called to *act* on this Truth and walk in him. As the book of James attests to brilliantly and brutally:

> Do not merely listen to the word, and so deceive your-
> selves. Do what it says. Anyone who listens to the word but
> does not do what it says is like someone who looks at his face
> in a mirror and, after looking at himself, goes away and
> immediately forgets what he looks like. But whoever looks
> intently into the perfect law that gives freedom, and continues
> in it – not forgetting what they have heard, but doing it –
> they will be blessed in what they do.
> (James 1:22–25)

What we listen to we need to act on.

CONFESSING TRUTH

In 1 John 1:8 we are told, 'If we claim to be without sin, we deceive ourselves and the truth is not in us.' This calls all followers, then and now, to walk in the truth, the light, because God is in the light and in him there is no darkness. How often have we wanted to minimize our shortcomings and character failures? We fear being exposed. We want to present passion, not poverty. This is nothing new. Ever since the garden of Eden, we have hidden in creation fearing exposure, humiliation and shame. Our current post-truth-dominated society is just another outworking of this; we are tempted to use our feelings to justify our behaviours: 'Did you see what he made me do?' 'How dare you say that! You have no idea what I am going through right now!' We lean on our own sense of self-justification and that in turn leads us to an elevated sense of self. At the heart of the 'my way or the highway' approach is an attitude of pride. Pride often emerges when we fear exposure. Pride bigs us up because we're scared of being found to be small.

In 1 John, we're reminded that we do not need to fear exposure. Confession is one of the ways we know truth is in us. Far from a stirring up of all things bad, a shameful thing to do, confession is a good, liberating and life-giving thing! To admit that we lie, distort truth and self-justify allows us to acknowledge the bad, because in repentance (seeking to turn away actively from this again in the future and instead turn towards Christ), we proclaim our need for a Saviour, Truth, and he meets us with grace, grace and more grace. Better to be a free and passionate pauper than a prideful person reliant on our self-sufficiency. We know from people who 'have it all' but don't know Jesus that this is just not enough. Comedian and actor Jim Carrey is often quoted as saying, 'I think everybody should get rich and famous and do everything they ever dreamed of so they can see that's not the answer.' As Jesus so wonderfully tells us in Mark 8:35: 'For whoever wants to save their life will lose it, but whoever loses their life for me and for the gospel will save it.' Confession shows our insufficiency to save ourselves and through it we acknowledge and walk in the truth.

OBEDIENT TRUTH

There is also another tension in 1 John: if we know him, we obey: 'We know that we have come to know him if we keep his commands. Whoever says, "I know him," but does not do what he commands is a liar, and the truth is not in that person" (1 John 2:3–4). Knowing Christ leads to obedience. This does not make us immune to sin, as we saw in the last section. But we are still called to obey Christ by keeping his commands, confession and forgiveness making it possible when we fall short (which we will).

In our often 'anything goes' age, obedience is seen as the ultimate restriction to our free will. But we frequently forget to look at *who* we are obeying. In this case, Truth is no fallible person and we are obeying Truth himself. Obeying this Truth may lead us into hard places and, as we have seen, many are unwilling to go there. But if we believe Christ is Truth himself, we know that obeying him will only lead to a more truthful way of life. Indeed, Jesus promises that he came so that we 'may have life, and have it to the full' (John 10:10). In 1 Peter 1:22–23, Peter ties unity (love for one another) to 'obeying the truth', which is found in the enduring Word of God, the gospel: Christ's gospel. This unity isn't found in us. The purification of our souls by our obedience to the truth (1 Peter 1:22) leads to and demands love for others. Obedience, then, isn't an ugly word. It's a beautiful word of truthful, life-giving vivacity, but it is a difficult word for some. Arguably, no more so than when it comes to sex.

Today, sex sells. It's on our TVs, in advertising and in culture's go-home-on-the-third-date rule. Regular sex is almost seen as the right of our generation. So, for any Christian wanting to be out in the world enjoying and engaging in culture, to obey Christ's word on sexual activity can cause a problem. Once again, Christ's word on the matter doesn't leave much room for 'my truth, your truth, his word, her word'. If we believe Christ is the Truth, then his teaching must also be the truth. Paul exhorts the Corinthians, a really diverse, contemporary mega church with all the spiritual gifts you could ask for, to 'Flee from sexual immorality' (1 Corinthians 6:18). Some Christians have been guilty of taking this teaching and warping it to believe that sex is bad. But God never said that. God designed sex and it was good. *Very* good. God loves sex. It was his idea, he created it and it is a gift to those of us who are married. For those of us who are single, though, we can be even more tempted to doubt that God's Word on the matter can really lead to our joy. No more so than when he says through Paul we are to avoid anything to do with sexual immorality, because the 'body . . . is not meant for sexual immorality but for the Lord, and the Lord for the body' (1 Corinthians 6:13). The purpose of our lives isn't to find 'the one', but to serve the Lord. And, remarkably, the Lord is also *for* our bodies: our Christian life is profoundly physical (see p. 86).

We are all sexual beings and we are all sexual sinners, whether in thought or word or deed. And yet, if God designed us this way and designed us to walk in the truth, we must obey what he says, even in the face of a cultural movement that might not.

However, God doesn't require us to do anything that he does not provide support for. His helper, the Spirit of Truth, works in us and through us to help shape our wills and desires. His voice is truth and we must follow him, even in the most counter-cultural of arenas, from sex to money to power and possessions, all of which we are bombarded with and told we need day after day. But we don't need to dwell in despair: we have the truth all these desires seek and later we'll look at how to share it.

WALKING IN TRUTH: COMMUNITY

Community lies at the heart of the Christian faith. It is there in the Trinity of Father, Son and Holy Spirit, three persons, one God, and it is there in God's plan for reaching his lost daughters and sons: the church. In our walk as Christians in the truth, it is of vital

It is God's will that you should be sanctified: that you should avoid sexual immorality; that each of you should learn to control your own body in a way that is holy and honorable, not in passionate lust like the pagans, who do not know God . . . Therefore, anyone who rejects this instruction does not reject a human being but God, the very God who gives you his Holy Spirit.

(1 Thessalonians 4:3–5, 8)

importance to know we are not alone, nor were we designed to do it alone. We are to 'encourage one another and build each other up' (1 Thessalonians 5:11). We are to encourage one another in the truth.

First, this means that objective creedal statements that stand firm throughout history are important, whether we love them or not! To some of us they may seem irrelevant, dry and dusty. In fact, I can remember church leaders saying to me when asked to sign the doctrinal basis before they spoke at an interdenominational event: 'My faith cannot be summed up by doctrinal statements. It's my relationship with God that matters, not a piece of paper.' I wonder if you can relate to that? Our suspicion over truth claims rears its head once more. Even as Christians, we do not like to be confined to boxes of belief. We prefer a dynamic, spontaneous relationship with God to the rigid, fusty details of doctrine. God is alive. That piece of paper isn't. One problem with this approach is that we must ask: what is the Bible? The Bible contains declarations of faith, even doctrines (see p. 88).

Most of these bad boys were drawn up at a time when the church was under theological attack from those seeking to undermine a mega-important part of who Jesus is, or what he has done. As we navigate what it looks like to walk in Truth as well as listen to him, these statements help us to know what to believe and why. We may be tempted to consider them as passes to indoctrinate the masses or even to undermine our personal relationship with God.

For what I received I passed on to you as of first importance: that Christ died for our sins according to the Scriptures, that he was buried, that he was raised on the third day according to the Scriptures.

(1 Corinthians 15:3–4)

But, far from that, they have been passed down by eye witnesses and, in some cases, then further articulated and clarified so that the church could succinctly know how best to defend itself against lies. That is why a doctrinal basis is a really good idea: it articulates core beliefs. As Director of the Universities and Colleges Christian Fellowship (and my former employer) Richard Cunningham used to say: 'The doctrinal basis is as broad as it can be, while being as narrow as the Bible allows.'

In our post-truth, feelings-led society, though, Christians can often mumble an apology for our inflexible views, much as some of us do with sex. It's as if we've somehow lost sight of the fact that what is true and good for us must be true and good for our friends! I was reminded of this recently when one of my friends asked to come along with me to a Church of England service. 'OK!' I replied sunnily, racking my brain as to whether or not this was the week of the genealogies, the massacre of the Canaanites or the bit about women eating their children. As my friend stood beside me, I was acutely aware of all the weird things Christians do. We stood up, then we sat down. We stood up again. We said the Nicene Creed. We sat down. We stood up. We sang a few songs. We sat down again. There was talk about drinking wine and blood and eating bread and flesh. When it was all finally over, I breathed a massive sigh of relief, apologies spilling from my lips as we sipped on weak squash, and I steered her towards the most 'normal' Christians I knew. I was in for a shock. You can imagine my surprise later that evening as we cruised through McDonald's drive-thru (my desperate last-ditch attempt at damage control) and she said to me she thought the creeds were credible not cultish. She'd never felt so loved, accepted and welcome. She was moved by what we said together as one church before God. She found communion an act of belonging and identity. I nearly spilt my Diet Coke all over the steering wheel! The creeds had done a great job of sharing with my friend what we believed. And she loved it!

The problem with *our* creeds is that in deciding what 'we' believe, we can, of course (and do!), differ in our opinions. Of primary importance is understanding the truth as it pertains to salvation. All other matters, from different beliefs on the spiritual gifts, the role of women and church government, we can debate and freely disagree on in unity. Church should be a safe place where we can work out truth and how we walk in it, regardless of gender, ethnicity, age and sexuality. We should all love one another in pursuit of the truth. And although all are welcome as they are, we cannot come to Christ and remain unchanged.

He was a murderer from the beginning, not holding to the truth, for there is no truth in him. When he lies, he speaks his native language, for he is a liar and the father of lies.

(John 8:44b)

Chapter ten

TESTING TRUTH – LIES AND DISCERNMENT

You may have seen the 2016 film *Denial*. The story focuses on the fight of Deborah Lipstadt, an American historian, who wrote *Denying the Holocaust*. In the book, she accuses revisionist historian David Irving of trying to show that the Holocaust didn't happen by falsifying evidence. Irving sued Lipstadt, along with Penguin Books, for libel. What followed was an arduous legal process whereby the burden of proof rested on Lipstadt under English law. In the end, she and her legal team won the case by using the justification defence: they demonstrated that Lipstadt's remarks were not libellous but substantively true. Irving *is* a Holocaust denier. Even though he consistently also denied this throughout the trial, at the end of the film, there is an exquisite moment when the actress playing Lipstadt, Rachel Weisz, looks at the camera and says:

> Freedom of speech means you can say whatever you want. What you can't do is lie and expect not to be held accountable for it. Not all opinions are equal. And some things happened, just like we say they do. Slavery happened, the

Black Death happened. The Earth is round, the ice caps are melting and Elvis is not alive.

Discerning between truth and lies, fact and fiction, is of paramount importance. In Lipstadt's case, this was the difference between denying the systematic killing of millions of Jews during Second World War by the Nazi machine, or saying these events were open to interpretation; there is evidence that it likely did not happen. Not all opinions, however, *are* equal. There is truth and there are lies. To deny the Holocaust is to lie about history. Even though the judge landed on a very clear verdict, if such a high-profile court case demanded so much scrutiny to arrive at the truth as to whether millions were exterminated *en masse*, we can be forgiven for wondering, 'How am I ever going to get to the truth in my own life?'

While society wants to fudge these two categories of truth and lies into an interpretative mess, Jesus very clearly calls out the difference between them. He says it is the difference between belonging to Satan or belonging to the Truth.

Throughout the Bible, we see that whatever Satan does is a desperate attempt to mirror God's activity. But his is a counterfeit. In Revelation, for example, we see Satan's demonic activity in producing the unholy trinity: the dragon, the beast and the false prophet (Revelation 16:13). Satan and his demonic hoard wage war on the saints, whereas God and his angels serve the saints. The mark of the beast in Revelation 13:18 is a demonic rip-off of the seal of the Spirit placed on believers (Ephesians 1:13). Whatever God does, Satan wants to distort or destroy. Their purposes are diametrically opposed to each other. One is good and the other is evil. One is Truth, the other is lies. This is what Jesus reminds us of in John 8: Satan does not hold to the truth. He is a liar. He is *the* liar. And so are all who belong to him. And yet, good is stronger than evil. Truth obliterates lies.

Earlier in John 8, Jesus says a number of crucial things. Some Jews 'who had believed' Jesus (John 8:31) began to question him when he claimed that the truth would set them free. What kind of freedom do they need? Does Jesus not know that they are descendants of Abraham? Surely that's enough? Jesus replies:

> everyone who sins is a slave to sin . . . I know that you are Abraham's descendants. Yet you are looking for a way to kill me, because you have no room for my word. I am telling you what I have seen in the Father's presence, and you are doing what you have heard from your father.
> (John 8:34, 37–38)

The Jews were quite pleased with this, thinking that finally Jesus got that Abraham was their father. Abraham was the one they listened to: '"Abraham is our father," they answered' (John 8:39). But this isn't the father Jesus was referring to. Jesus challenges them again, denying that they are Abraham's children because, if they were, Abraham would have listened to Jesus, whereas they are plotting to kill him. No, Jesus says, 'You are doing the works of your own father' (John 8:41).

But *who* is their father? If Jesus isn't referring to their ancestor Abraham, then who does he mean? The suspense continues to build as once more the Jews cry out in outrage, 'We are not illegitimate children . . . The only Father we have is God himself' (John 8:41). Ergo, 'What right do you have to speak to us? We do not recognize your authority, Jesus of Nazareth.' Jesus then said to them:

> If God were your Father, you would love me, for I have come here from God. I have not come on my own; God sent me. Why is my language not clear to you? Because you are unable to hear what I say.
> (John 8:42)

The big reveal comes next (see opposite).

As the ruling Jews begin to plot the death of Jesus, Jesus says they belong to the one who was a murderer from the beginning, Satan himself. Satan does not listen to the truth either. There is zero truth in him whatsoever. So, it's no wonder they do not recognize Truth when he speaks to them. They belong to the devil, not to God. See p. 98 for what Jesus goes on to say.

You belong to your father, the devil, and you want to carry out your father's desires. He was a murderer from the beginning, not holding to the truth, for there is no truth in him. When he lies, he speaks his native language, for he is a liar and the father of lies.

(John 8:44)

Yet because I tell the truth, you do not believe me! Can any of you prove me guilty of sin? If I am telling the truth, why don't you believe me? Whoever belongs to God hears what God says. The reason you do not hear is that you do not belong to God.

(John 8:45–47)

Such binary statements make us squirm a bit. It cannot be that clear cut. As we have already seen, there is a belonging dimension when it comes to truth. Relational as truth is, we relate to the truth; we *belong* to it. The flip side of this is that it's the same when it comes to lies.

The father of lies wants to deceive the world. As the famous quote from *The Usual Suspects* goes, 'The greatest trick the devil ever pulled was convincing the world he didn't exist.' And he wants to deceive Christians as much as he can too. It began in the garden, but it continues today. As Peter exhorts scattered, suffering Christians, so he exhorts us: 'Be alert and of sober mind. Your enemy the devil prowls around like a roaring lion looking for someone to devour' (1 Peter 5:8). Again, in Ephesians we are told to 'take up the shield of faith, with which you can extinguish all the flaming arrows of the evil one' (Ephesians 6:16).

FAITH VERSUS FLAMING ARROWS

As we have seen, the evil one wants to derail us, wants to deceive us and wants us to denounce Christ. He wants to pollute our minds with lies and error, to drag us away from the truth and the light of Christ's kingdom into the darkness of his dominion. As Paul once again reminds us in Ephesians, 'For our struggle is not against flesh and blood, but against the rulers, against the authorities, against the powers of this dark world and against the spiritual forces of evil in the heavenly realms' (Ephesians 6:12).

Our struggle is against the spiritual forces of evil. As we navigate what it means to know truth in an 'anything goes' age, we must remember that behind every ruler, every author, every film, every government, every country that seeks to suppress truth is the father of all lies. And every tug we feel on our hearts to suppress truth through what we read, think, watch, do and say is from the father of all lies. From the verses we've seen above, this is something the biblical authors were more than aware of, but they were not afraid of him. With every word of warning to watch out comes a remedy: 'be alert and of sober mind' (1 Peter 5:8), 'take up the shield of faith' (Ephesians 6:16) and 'Finally, be strong in the Lord and in his mighty power. Put on the full armor of God, so that you can take your stand against the devil's schemes' (Ephesians 6:10–11).

The way we discern lies is by focusing not on them but on the truth. It is as we soak ourselves in the truth of Christ that we more readily identify lies. If the Jews Jesus was talking with had really understood Abraham and what he was pointing to, they would have embraced Christ as the object of Abraham's faith. If they were rooted in the truth, they would have recognized error. It's the same with us. If you, like many, find reading the Bible challenging, it can be tempting to pursue God's truth primarily through your prayer life. However, it is in God's written Word, the Bible, that we can learn more about his steadfast nature, his heart, his will, enabling us to pray and understand him better.

Paul says we are to put on Jesus' full armour of faith, truth, right-eousness, gospel of peace, salvation and the Spirit. But as we put these things on, Paul doesn't then say, 'And now to go to war against the father of lies!' Instead, four times in Ephesians 6, Paul tells the church to 'stand' (verse 13), 'stand firm' (verse 14), 'stand your ground' (verse 13) and 'stand against' (verse 11). We fight lies by standing in the truth. Standing firm. And we stand firm by actively calling to mind and physically walking in the truth of the gospel; in our listening and our doing. Paul wants to remind us that our strength in the Lord comes from his mighty power; all that he has achieved for us through the cross. We extinguish Satan's flaming arrows of deceitful lies not by turning to fight him but by actively standing firm in our faith in Truth himself.

With such a clear distinction between truth and lies, it may be tempting to think the cosmic battle is a bit like the situation in *Star Wars*: equal forces locked head to head in a battle between good and evil. But, spoiler alert, there wasn't and never will be any doubt about who triumphs and wins the day. The biblical picture of good and evil is not one where these co-eternal, external forces fight it out to the bitter end. As one of the Reformers once said of Satan, 'Even the devil is God's devil' (Martin Luther). He is a created, spiritual being with no existence outside what God allows for him.

THE SPIRIT OF TRUTH

At a basic level the distinction between truth and lies is simple: Truth is Jesus, lies are the devil. But in the day-to-day working out of our faith, it can be so difficult to discern the truth. The devil just loves to whisper in our ears, 'You're not good enough, Jesus isn't enough', to steer us out of truth's course. Thankfully, we are not left alone to discern the voice of truth. We are given an aid to help us. Before Jesus is led away to his execution, he comforts his disciples by promising a Truth-Helper (see opposite).

This Spirit of Truth, Christ's Spirit, the Truth-Helper, is a person who Jesus says will do three things (see p. 104).

For me, these are among the most beautiful words in Scripture. Jesus says his Truth-Helper is going to convict the world concerning sin, righteousness and judgment. This is how the Spirit speaks truth. He convicts the world of sin; he shows the world its need for forgiveness in Jesus. He convicts the world of righteousness. It is because we do not see Truth face to face right now that we need the Spirit to convict us of Christ's righteousness, his sinlessness, which is then credited to us. So the Father views us as Christ himself, without sin or stain. Jesus says the Spirit of Truth will convict us of this truth because Jesus isn't here to do it. The Spirit also convicts us concerning judgment: Satan's time is up, our struggle against lies is limited, Christ has come to 'destroy the devil's work' (1 John 3:8) and he does this ultimately and definitively

The Spirit searches all things, even the deep things of God. For who knows a person's thoughts except their own spirit within them? In the same way no one knows the thoughts of God except the Spirit of God. What we have received is not the spirit of the world, but the Spirit who is from God, so that we may understand what God has freely given us. This is what we speak, not in words taught us by human wisdom but in words taught by the Spirit, explaining spiritual realities with Spirit-taught words.

(1 Corinthians 2:10b–13)

When he comes, he will prove the world to be in the wrong about sin and righteousness and judgment: about sin, because people do not believe in me; about righteousness, because I am going to the Father, where you can see me no longer; and about judgment, because the prince of this world now stands condemned.

(John 16:8–11)

by paying our debt for sin on the cross. Like Rachel Weisz's words in *Denial*, 'What you cannot do is lie and expect not to be held accountable for it', the devil will be held accountable for all his lies, from leading Adam and Eve to their deaths to leading many in society away from truth.

As we journey in truth, we have the Spirit of Truth filling us. Jesus says: 'He [the Spirit] will glorify me, for he will take what is mine and declare it to you. All that the Father has is mine; therefore, I said that he will take what is mine and declare it to you' (John 16:14). All that belongs to Jesus belongs to us as we belong to truth. His Truth-Helper applies all that is Christ's to us: we can even call his Father our Father. Truth's Sonship is our sonship, his Spirit is now ours in us: 'the Spirit you received brought about your adoption to sonship. And by him we cry, "*Abba*, Father"' (Romans 8:15b).

In our confusion-rife society, day to day it can be easy to forget this adoption, that all that belongs to Jesus is ours. Not fully grasping this, there is often a fear that surrounds our decision making when it comes to following God's will for us: am I sure that's what God is saying? What if I've got it all wrong? Too often, this fear can lead us to ruminate upon our decisions, pros and cons lists at the ready, rather than turning to the most practical lie-buster we have at our disposal: we discern lies by dwelling on the truth (because we are already united in and to the Truth!). Like any relationship, the more you spend time with someone, the more you learn that person's voice, thoughts and preferences. The most proactive thing you can do to know the Truth is to spend time with him through his Word. But here are a couple of other ways we can better discern between the truth and lies.

Speak truth over ourselves and others

The book of Ephesians tells us to 'Stand firm then, with the belt of truth buckled around your waist, with the breastplate of righteousness in place' (6:14). One way we can ensure we are putting on our armour of God is to actively buckle that belt! We can ask God which lies we have been believing and then we can ask a friend to speak the truth over us. They can speak truths that particularly relate to the lie we have believed, but they could also bring to bear wider, bigger truths in Christ: you are loved, you are known, you are not alone. We don't want to speak clichés or platitudes but apply the Scriptures to one another's hearts. Read out Paul's prayers for the church collectively or to one another. Read out Ephesians 1 and insert your name in the gaps: '*Josh*, you have redemption through his blood . . . You, *Sophie*, were included in Christ when you heard the message of truth.' Yes, Ephesians 1 deliberately speaks of 'us', the corporate church, and all *we* have *in* Christ, but as long as we don't teach that it was written purely for the Sophies and Joshes of this world, it is a powerful means of personally reminding ourselves of what we corporately share in Christ. It's also a significant way in which our faith grows and the Spirit presses Christ into our hearts.

This is precisely what happens when the church gathers together and sings to God and to one another. The danger for conservatives is that we may feel like spectators, looking on while we sing *at* God, and for charismatics, we may well feel as though we are *only* singing to God.

Test the spirits

John encourages us to test what we receive: 'Dear friends, do not believe every spirit, but test the spirits to see whether they are from God, because many false prophets have gone out into the world' (1 John 4:1). We can test truth in our age of scepticism by testing the spirits. This does not mean we doubt because we do not think it is possible to know, as sceptics hold. Instead, we are called to *question* because we do know the truth. It has been set before us clearly in the Scriptures. Whatever we hear, read and experience is to be weighed against the Scriptures. As our struggle is against powers of the evil one and his flaming darts, his demonic spirits are part of that struggle. They want to lead us away with fine-sounding arguments or even through false teaching in the churches. As we measure all we encounter against the external Word of God, we are able to discern and test whether or not the message is from God. What God upholds in his Word he will not undo through other messages, either from the world or within the church, particularly if we are prophetic keenos! If we believe this is an ongoing work of the Spirit (depending upon how we define this too), then any words of knowledge or prophecy we may receive are to be brought to the normative standard of Scripture and measured. For example, in his first letter to the church in Corinth, Paul explains, 'But the one who prophesies speaks to people for their strengthening, encouraging and comfort' (1 Corinthians 14:3). This does not mean prophecies may not challenge us or stretch our spiritual muscle, but if a prophecy does not ultimately accord to Scripture and strengthen, encourage or comfort us, then we can know it is not the truth. The same logic can apply in other situations. Testing is not a sign of spiritual weakness. It is, in fact, a sign of alive and active faith. Another example of this would be testing the teaching we receive each week at church from the front, and through various other channels throughout the week. Are we receiving the truth of God's Word?

Make disciples of all nations, baptizing them in the name of the Father and of the Son and of the Holy Spirit, and teaching them to obey everything I have commanded you. And surely I am with you always, to the very end of the age.

(Matthew 28:19–20)

Chapter eleven

TALKING TRUTH – ENGAGING THE APATHETIC, SCEPTICAL AND TRUTH-SEEKERS

I was on a train travelling from Vienna to Budapest. Usually I really enjoy these journeys as an opportunity for reflection, watching the landscape change from the structured borders of Austria to the rolling fields of Hungary. But this time my reflection wasn't quite so silent: there were two other people in our carriage.

My travelling companions were from Canada, and we had an excellent two and a half hours together, exchanging holiday stories, talking about cuisine and politics.

'Trump is a d★★k!' one of my new friends exclaimed as the carriage doors burst open and three Americans squeezed into our compartment. What followed was a delightful conversation about family, careers and life experience. But, as we listened intently, the elephant sat quietly, a book written by one of Trump's former campaign directors tucked neatly under one of the American's arms. None of us brought it up.

The moment our three fellow travellers alighted, one of the Canadians confirmed, 'Yeah, definite Trump supporters.' We knew it. But what was the point in talking about awkward differences of opinion, things we were never going to agree on?

The thing is, this is often how we feel when it comes to sharing truth. Truth becomes the awkward elephant in the conversation. Your friends or others may know that you're a Christian but you don't really want to bring it up, especially not now, especially when you may be met with either violent, opposing ideas, stereotypes or just plain apathy. 'Truth? Ha. Don't you know there is no such thing as black and white?' The elephant sits quietly or is quickly brought up centre stage, then even more quickly dismissed.

How do we become truth-tellers in our carriages of life (as Matthew 28:16–20) when we are surrounded by different, often opposing ideas and values? How do we speak of truth in a meaningful way?

KNOW THE TIMES

Truth didn't come to us in a vacuum. It's the reason this book is looking at *our* uncertain world. Truth came to us with flesh on, in time and space, so we could understand him. As one of my former colleagues once wrote, 'the incarnation is the greatest act of persuasion'. The way in which we can speak meaningfully about truth is for us to understand the ways truth is understood in our culture today. A great way of doing this is by reading the BBC headlines online, having a listen to the charts and seeing who the winners of the Man Booker Prize and others are. Listen to what society is 'incarnating'. What does our society listen to and, therefore, speak of? For example, truth for many today is to 'be happy'. As long as I am happy and I don't hurt anyone, that is *my* truth. It doesn't matter if it's true for you too. If truth equals happiness, we and others will jettison any notions of truth that contradict our happiness. It's important we understand this in our conversations.

Or how about love, the incessant pursuit of romantic relationships, as today's truth? You will be satisfied when you find 'the one'. That is the truth of life. It's not Jesus saying I am the Way, the Truth and the Life, it is sex and relationships. Finding that other person who completes you. He or she may not be perfect but wants you, and that's what matters.

It doesn't take much digging for us to see how dissatisfactory this actually is: for ourselves and for others. But it's in this understanding of desires and through empathizing with the dissatisfaction that we can start to talk about truth in Christ. The reality is that no-one is that apathetic because God has written eternity on our hearts (Ecclesiastes 3:11). And it's through exposing these desires, these frameworks of life and meaning (world views), that we can speak the truth of Christ. No-one is neutral. They are wedded to something or someone.

So before talking about the truth, understand the underlying assumptions, values and ideas of the person you are speaking with. What are they? How can you find out? Our times as a whole give us a good indicator, but understanding cultural values is no substitute for understanding the unique person before you. In an age of relative truth, each person will hold something different, or may have a slightly different, nuanced understanding of it. Let's not be quick to assume the rhetoric of militant atheists, thinking our friends share the same thought processes. John Gray's book *Seven Types of Atheism* is a brilliant way of understanding how atheist thinking has developed and splintered off.

Here are a few example ways to ask 'how do you know that?' in conversations (borrowed from Randy Newman's *Questioning Evangelism*):

> 'What makes you believe that?'
> 'What convinces you of that?'
> 'Where have you heard that?'
> 'What is the strongest case for that?'
> 'Has someone persuaded you of this perspective?'
> 'Have you read some things that have sold you on this?'

Questions, revealing as the answers may be, will only get us so far. Jesus asked over 300 questions throughout the gospels. He loved using them. They expose, clarify and serve the person you are speaking with beautifully. Jesus, however, didn't just ask questions. He also *lived out* the truth. In so many instances, the Pharisees picked on Jesus for eating and drinking with tax collectors and sinners. He was called a glutton and a drunk! But they observed how he acted on the sabbath and how he treated women and social outcasts. Jesus preached the truth, asked questions to create space in hearts into which the truth could land and he lived out the truth.

Authenticity and experience are (for many of us, at least) our values. We can see through lies, masks and pretence at a glance. So can our friends. Meaningfully sharing truth is the union of both objective and subjective knowledge. It means we know the truth and we walk in the truth. When it comes to sharing the truth, we share it as we walk in it. Anything else is hypocrisy and our friends are too clever to buy it. We don't need to hide behind false perfection or layers of 'sortedness'. If we believe the gospel is good news for sinners, we can freely share our own need before others.

The way we cut through cynicism, pretence and manipulation, the effects of post-truth, is to be transparent. Ask for forgiveness. Let's own our messiness and mistakes, being distinctive in how we rejoice in the truth that has set us free from shame. This is how we share truth in a way that connects with others. We display the truth setting us free *today*. Our testimonies of how we originally received Christ are important and precious, but we can often neglect what he is doing in us right now. Or we can be so focused on what he is doing right now that we lose sight of what he has done once and for all for us.

KNOW YOUR LIFE AND MAKE THE MOST OF IT

This means we want to identify not only what culture is living out, but what we are living out! Where you are now is where God has placed you to be the best woman or man of God you can possibly be. Where are you? Single? Married? Divorced? Widowed? Children? Childless? Student? At work? At home? In between? Unemployed?

What are your daily rhythms and how can you bring others into them? Through a coffee break? Or dinner with your housemates? Or a quick lunch while the kids are sleeping? How can you make the most of your daily rhythms in such a way that you can invite others in and live before them and with them? This will look different from person to person and there will be a whole load of minutiae to consider, but the challenge is an important one: who are you going out to in order to bring in?

TRUTHFUL EVIDENCE

Jesus' disciple, Thomas, remains our friend when it comes to us speaking the truth. Not only is he bold (and maybe stupid!)

enough to ask Jesus, 'What is the way?', he also misses out on the initial resurrection appearance of Jesus. He hears it second hand. Again, he is challenged and not by accident. Will he believe that Jesus is the way on the basis of second-hand testimony? He doesn't. He adamantly insists that he has to see 'his hands and his side'. And the great thing is that Jesus says, 'OK!' Jesus honours the place and role of evidence in our faith-forming. He allows Thomas to come to him and place his hands in his wounds and his side. He does not say, 'Thomas, you should know by now' (though he should know!). In humility, Jesus honours his request and asks Thomas to come to him.

The role of evidence is, therefore, an important one. We and others aren't asked to believe in truth on the basis of blind faith, wishful thinking or psychological Freudian projection of an innate need for a daddy in the sky. Jesus says, 'Look at me. Touch me. Now what do you think?'

In our truth-telling, we want to be able to articulate the beauty and significance of truth, but we can also present the evidence. The eye-witness accounts of Jesus' life are prime examples of historical evidence. Many may write them off, believing them to be biased, but biographies that include the personal failures of those who wrote them don't seem to be manipulated documents written for personal gain. They are written so 'you may know the truth/be convinced/believe'. And there is so much more evidence besides! Check out the significance of the Cyrus Cylinder and the

Nineveh reliefs at the British Museum. This is just the tip of the iceberg. Belief comes through faith and this faith is entirely reasonable, even if we don't have absolute proof for everything we believe. We can't press our hands into Truth's wounds as Thomas did, but we are given access to Thomas's experience. Jesus says, 'blessed are those who have not seen and yet have believed' (John 20:29b). We are even more blessed downstream from Jesus, not seeing him yet believing, not in spite of the evidence but in accordance with it.

So, what kind of evidence are your friends looking for? Ask them. If they dodge the question by saying, 'Oh, I'd believe if God were to stand in front of me and tell me personally', they may be thinking that the existence of Truth is such an extraordinary claim that it demands extraordinary evidence. Here are a few things you can work into the conversation in response.

1 Anything you don't know could count as an extraordinary claim, like quantum mechanics. Yet this seems to be widely accepted. Why do you think that is? The statement 'extraordinary claims require extraordinary evidence' is itself an extraordinary assertion! Where is the extraordinary evidence that we should believe such a claim? Please could you show me the extraordinary evidence that makes this claim true?

2 What counts as an extraordinary claim depends on what you know or don't know. The parameters as to what constitutes 'extraordinary' will change from person to person and they're

even subject to change personally. At one point, quantum mechanics (or the Higgs boson) was seen as an extraordinary claim, but it then transpired that it wasn't and these things are now commonly held. So something else then shifts into the bracket of 'extraordinary claims'. As extraordinary claims keep shifting and different people demand different types of evidence based on their knowledge, wouldn't you want confidence that God exists? Evidence that is reliable and true?

3 I'm glad you asked! The kind of evidence Truth makes available to us that is reliable and true are the documents on his life and death. The reason Truth makes himself known through these written accounts in the Bible is because they provide us with a permanent witness. If God were to reveal himself to you and tell you he exists, you may still believe it in your incredulity a couple of hours later. But what about the following morning? I imagine thoughts like 'Did that really happen?' and 'Did I eat or drink anything unusual beforehand?' would start spinning through our heads. And then, when we tried to share this experience with others, what would they say? 'Ah yeah, well, I'd believe that happened to you if it also happened to me!' Do we see the problem? Truth has made himself universally available to people through the permanent and true accounts of his life. Truth has spoken to us. And we can remember those accounts by looking at them again the following day! Isn't that something you would want to experience?

4 They may well respond, 'Yes, but only if it is actually God speaking to me through these documents.' Or, 'Yes, if the accounts are actually reliable.' If that is the case, you know what to do. If they don't want to engage, that's OK. Truth knows and loves them more than we do. The truth will out. Be patient, keep praying and perhaps say to them, 'Please keep thinking about it. I won't bring this up each time we see each other, but if you'd like to talk about it, you know I'm here. Truth is important for both of us. I hope we'll be able to chat about this again. If you'd like to, you could come with me to church one Sunday and see what it looks like to know God for yourself.' We don't want to be prescriptive; we want to be personal. But if we aren't sure what to say, this is one way I talk with some of my friends about truth. Inviting friends into the personal context of church community serves to undercut any suspicions of power play as they see love in action. They are able to see what it looks like to know Jesus reliably, and they may very well encounter God for themselves as they hear his word taught and experience the quality of Christian relationship.

STANDING BEHIND YOUR WORDS (SPEAKING AND STANDING IN TRUTH)

In our age of change and flux, let's be those who stand behind our words. May our yes be yes and our no be no (Matthew 5:37). The flipflopping of politics, ever-changing statements from potential perpetrators of abuse and the truthful abusive reality of those famed for their altruism make us and others suspicious of Christians. How can we trust? By being followers of truth who stand behind our words is one significant way. As we demonstrate our reliability and trustworthiness, we also demonstrate the reliable character and trustworthiness of truth. This will not go unnoticed. What does it look like for you to stand by your words as you stand in the Word this week?

TRUTH-TELLING TRULY HUMAN IMAG(IN)ERS

Jesus shows us what it means to be truly human. He is the image of God reflecting what it means to demonstrate God to others. This is why the unity between heads and hearts, objective and subjective is so important. As the author of *A Wrinkle in Time*, Madeleine L'Engle, shares in another book called *The Rock that Is Higher*:

> Jesus taught by telling stories, parables, myths, and his stories were true, though not everybody could hear them. Jesus came to show us through his stories what it is to be human and what it is to be heroic and to understand heroes.

Jesus sparks interest and imagination. By using stories, he invites the hearer to place themselves into the scene. Some understand the subversive nature of what he is saying and walk to him. Others understand and they walk away. Either way, Jesus uses the creative powers of the imagination to harness the interest and engagement of his hearers. He is able to sneak past the 'watchful dragons' and enter hearts (see C. S. Lewis, *On Stories*). The way we tell truth as truly human imag(in)ers reflects to others what it means to represent God in all that we are and all that we have. This includes the use of imagination.

G. K. Chesterton, writer and philosopher, argued that the imagination is the solution to rationalism. The rationalists, he argued, are lunatics because they only believe themselves, locked into their rationalist rooms. Rather than joining them, meeting rationalism with rationalism, locked in there with them, we stand outside and show them a thicker, more full way of the world so that they may be enticed out. Rational capacity is only part of what it means to be made in the image of God. It is an interesting rational faith to possess that cannot explain love, joy, beauty, etc.

As truth-telling imag(in)ers, using our imaginations will help us to demonstrate the joy, love and high hope we have in truth. How do we use the imagination in our truth-telling? Well, you'd be surprised by how many rationalists are still lurking. And we can also just as easily sub out rationalism and send in scientific method or idealism or scepticism. Any of these theories of knowledge we looked at that rely on themselves in order to self-authenticate will have a hard time explaining something that doesn't come under their scope. What is love to the scientist? Is it purely a chemical reaction in the brain? How can we know our friends, family, partners, etc. actually love us? Do we insist we place their brains under a microscope or in an MRI machine to see the firings of their neuro-chemistry in order to prove they love us? Or do we take it on the basis of trust as seen in word and action? Understanding what our friends and others appeal to in order to know will enable us to unleash the imagination. We can paint pictures and scenes and ask them questions based on that. We can use the imagination to irritate investigation. It's also important for us to enjoy and harness the imagination for ourselves as we do this.

TRUTHFUL WITNESS

We are called to go out and make disciples. As Jesus commands the disciples in Matthew 28:16–20, so he commands us. It is a high privilege we have to be truth-tellers, telling the story of the True-Myth and demonstrating his truth in our lives as we personally love others and meet them where they are. This is the way Truth chooses to make himself known: through us. But the responsibility does not rest upon us to save. The beauty of the Great Commission is that Truth finishes these words saying that he will be with us to the very end of the age. To the end of our post-truth age or whatever we 'progress' into next, Truth comes with us. The Spirit of Truth abides in us so we can have great confidence in the work and words of Truth as well as the witness of his Spirit in us and through us. Truth does not leave us alone. Truth comes with us. Truth lives in us. Truth speaks for himself through his Word. We have the liberating privilege of being those who point to Truth.

Truth is real,
Truth has flesh,
Truth walked
among us.
And Truth's
name is
Jesus Christ.

Conclusion

THE QUEST FOR TRUTH COMPLETE IN CHRIST

Our age of uncertainty is searching for truth it can trust. And though it may look as if Jesus' claim to be the Truth has been dismissed, we have seen that ever since the garden, humanity has been searching to find it again; too often in all the wrong places. We have explored the false starts and dead ends of Descartes, Locke and Camus, and felt the continued weariness of our post-truth age, wondering if truth really is available to find.

And yet, our disappointment at a lack of truth has exposed our need for it. We are hungry for truth, hope and authentic, loving community. We are hungry for a better way. Jesus satisfies this hunger, promising that whoever 'comes to me will never go hungry' (John 6:35). Jesus is Truth; he is the Truth who anchors our longings and provides us with knowledge of him, leading to salvation and rest. *He* is our confident Truth in this uncertain world, until the very end (Matthew 28:20). Being known by him we are able to live and speak truth to a divided, increasingly tribal world. This isn't a knowing that cuts off heads from hearts but one that unites the two.

I pray we would be empowered to be that counter-cultural community of Truth-lovers, sharing the good news of his Truth-full gospel in all our weakness. Truth may well be an uncomfortable word to some, but let's demonstrate that it is the best word we could ever hope for because, in Jesus, all God's promises to us are 'Yes' and 'Amen' (2 Corinthians 2:10). Truth has arrived. We are no longer left in the dark. Truth is real, Truth has flesh, Truth walked among us. And Truth's name is Jesus Christ.

References

Eugène Delacroix, *The Journal of Eugène Delacroix* (London: Phaidon Press, 2001).

Madeleine L'Engle, *The Rock that Is Higher: Stories as Truth* (Colorado Springs, Colo.: WaterBrook Press, 2002).

Steven Garber, *Visions of Vocation: Common Grace for the Common Good* (Downers Grove, Ill.: InterVarsity Press, 2014).

John Gray, *Seven Types of Atheism* (London: Allen Lane, 2018).

The Guardian, 'Democracy at risk due to fake news and data misuse, MPs conclude', <https://www.theguardian.com/technology/2018/jul/27/fake-news-inquiry-data-misuse-deomcracy-at-risk-mps-conclude>, last accessed 13 November 2018.

C. S. Lewis, *The Lion, the Witch and the Wardrobe* (London: HarperCollins, 2001).

C. S. Lewis, 'Sometimes Fairy Stories May Say Best What's to Be Said' in *On Stories: And Other Essays on Literature* (San Diego, Calif.: Harcourt Brace Jovanovich, 1982).

Deborah Lipstadt, *Denying the Holocaust: The Growing Assault on Truth and Memory* (London: Penguin, 2016).

Randy Newman, *Questioning Evangelism: Engaging People's Hearts the Way Jesus Did* (Grand Rapids, Mich.: Kregel Publications, 2004).

Timothy Snyder, *On Tyranny: Twenty Lessons from the Twentieth Century* (London: Bodley Head, 2017).

George Steiner, *No Passion Spent: Essays 1978–1996* (London: Faber & Faber, 1996).

John Stott, *The Cross of Christ* (Nottingham: Inter-Varsity Press, 1989).

Acknowledgments

> Jesus did many other things as well. If every one of them were written down, I suppose that even the whole world would not have room for the books that would be written.
> (John 21:25)

I wish there were a little bit more room in this book.

There are too many friends vying for a place on this page to be able to mention everyone by name; you know who you are.

My first thanks go to Elizabeth Neep, my fab commissioning editor, for suggesting a little Skype chat way back when to discuss writing a book, and to our lovely mutual friend Eleanor Elms: thank you both for bearing with me, being ruthless and for your timely encouragements. You've picked me up when I've needed it most.

Thank you to my dear friend and ministry mate, Luke Cawley – your wisdom and humour have kept me buoyant – who knew writing a short book for a series could be so agonizing? A massive thank you goes to Mark Meynell for being my personal Greek lexicon, commentary, sounding board and agony aunt; having your eyes on this text gave me peace. I owe an equally large debt of gratitude to Tom Roberts, who, a few days before the final deadline, read through the entire draft, supplying me with oodles of notes, questions and thoughts to consider. Thank you for injecting and renewing my confidence in this project.

I am so thankful for my friends who have cheered me on, kept me sane and cooked me meals in the madness, especially as I've moved jobs (even cities) and started a PhD, and through all the other weird and wonderful things the Lord has entrusted me with these past 18 months – Emily, Rachel O., Sophie M., Sophie S., Josh J., Harriet D., Tim D., Rachel and Ben W., Ian R., Dawn E., Matt C., Adam C. and so many more! A huge thank you to Elizabeth Rudin, my mother, for so patiently leading me through my reluctance to the loving arms of Christ.

My final word of thanks goes to Truth himself: this book is limited, as I am, but, if it pleases you, weave these weak words into the hearts of those who need you the most.